D1242805

CALIBAN REBORN

Renewal in Twentieth-Century Music

WORLD PERSPECTIVES

Volumes already published

I	Approaches to God	Jacques Maritain
II	Accent on Form	Lancelot Law Whyte
III	Scope of Total Architecture	Walter Gropius
IV	Recovery of Faith	Sarvepalli Radhakrishnan
V	World Indivisible	Konrad Adenauer
VI	Society and Knowledge	V. Gordon Childe
VII	The Transformations of Man	Lewis Mumford
VIII	Man and Materialism	Fred Hoyle
IX	The Art of Loving	Erich Fromm
X	Dynamics of Faith	Paul Tillich
XI	Matter, Mind and Man	Edmund W. Sinnott
XII	Mysticism: Christian and Buddhist	Daisetz Teitaro Suzuki
XIII	Man's Western Quest	Denis de Rougemont
XIV	American Humanism	Howard Mumford Jones
XV	The Meeting of Love and Knowledge	Martin C. D'Arcy, S.J.
XVI	Rich Lands and Poor	Gunnar Myrdal
XVII	Hinduism: Its Meaning for the Liberation of the Spirit	Swami Nikhilananda
XVIII	Can People Learn to Learn?	Brock Chisholm
XIX	Physics and Philosophy	Werner Heisenberg
XX	Art and Reality	Joyce Cary
XXI	Sigmund Freud's Mission	Erich Fromm
XXII	Mirage of Health	René Dubos
XXIII	Issues of Freedom	Herbert J. Muller
XXIV	Humanism	Moses Hadas

tween subject and object; the indwelling of the one in the other. It interprets present and past events impinging on human life in our growing World Age and envisages what man may yet attain when summoned by an unbending inner necessity to the quest of what is most exalted in him. Its purpose is to offer new vistas in terms of world and human development while refusing to betray the intimate correlation between universality and individuality, dynamics and form, freedom and destiny. Each author deals with the increasing realization that spirit and nature are not separate and apart; that intuition and reason must regain their importance as the means of perceiving and fusing inner being with outer reality.

World Perspectives endeavors to show that the conception of wholeness, unity, organism is a higher and more concrete conception than that of matter and energy. Thus an enlarged meaning of life, of biology, not as it is revealed in the test tube of the laboratory but as it is experienced within the organism of life itself, is attempted in this Series. For the principle of life consists in the tension which connects spirit with the realm of matter, symbiotically joined. The element of life is dominant in the very texture of nature, thus rendering life, biology, a transempirical science. The laws of life have their origin beyond their mere physical manifestations and compel us to consider their spiritual source. In fact, the widening of the conceptual framework has not only served to restore order within the respective branches of knowledge, but has also disclosed analogies in man's position regarding the analysis and synthesis of experience in apparently separated domains of knowledge, suggesting the possibility of an ever more embracing objective description of the meaning of life.

Knowledge, it is shown in these books, no longer consists in a manipulation of man and nature as opposite forces, nor in the reduction of data to mere statistical order, but is a means of liberating mankind from the destructive power of fear, pointing the way toward the goal of the rehabilitation of the human will and the rebirth of faith and confidence in the human person. The works published also endeavor to reveal that the cry for patterns, systems and authorities is growing less insistent as the desire grows stronger in both East and West for the recovery of a dignity, integrity and self-realization which are the inalienable rights of man who may now guide change by means of conscious purpose in the light of rational experience.

The volumes in this Series endeavor to demonstrate that only in a society in which awareness of the problems of science exists, can its discoveries start great waves of change in human culture, and in such a manner that these discoveries may deepen and not erode the sense of universal human community. The differences in the disciplines, their epistemological exclusiveness, the variety of historical experiences, the differences of traditions, of cultures, of languages, of the arts, should be protected and preserved. But the interrelationship and unity of the whole should at the same time be accepted.

The authors of *World Perspectives* are of course aware that the ultimate answers to the hopes and fears which pervade modern society rest on the moral fibre of man, and on the wisdom and responsibility of those who promote the course of its development. But moral decisions cannot dispense with an insight into the interplay of the objective elements which offer and limit the choices made. Therefore an understanding of what the issues are, though not a sufficient condition, is a necessary prerequisite for directing action toward constructive solutions.

Other vital questions explored relate to problems of international understanding as well as to problems dealing with prejudice and the resultant tensions and antagonisms. The growing perception and responsibility of our World Age point to the new reality that the individual person and the collective person supplement and integrate each other; that the thrall of totalitarianism of both left and right has been shaken in the universal desire to recapture the authority of truth and human totality. Mankind can finally place its trust not in a proletarian authoritarianism, not in a secularized humanism, both of which have betrayed the spiritual property right of history, but in a sacramental brotherhood and in the unity of knowledge. This new consciousness has created a widening of human horizons beyond every parochialism, and a revolution in human thought comparable to the basic assumption, among the ancient Greeks, of the sovereignty of reason; corresponding to the great effulgence of the moral conscience articulated by the Hebrew prophets; analogous to the fundamental assertions of Christianity; or to the beginning of the new scientific era, the era of the science of dynamics, the experimental foundations of which were laid by Galileo in the Renaissance.

An important effort of this Series is to re-examine the contradictory meanings and applications which are given today to such terms as democracy, freedom, justice, love, peace, brotherhood and God. The purpose of such inquiries is to clear the way for the foundation of a genuine *world* history not in terms of nation or race or culture but in terms of man in relation to God, to himself, his fellow man and the universe, that reach beyond immediate self-interest. For the meaning of the World Age consists in respecting man's hopes and dreams which lead to a deeper understanding of the basic values of all peoples.

World Perspectives is planned to gain insight into the meaning of man, who not only is determined by history but who also determines history. History is to be understood as concerned not only with the life of man on this planet but as including also such cosmic influences as interpenetrate our human world. This generation is discovering that history does not conform to the social optimism of modern civilization and that the organization of human communities and the establishment of freedom and peace are not only intellectual achievements but spiritual and moral achievements as well, demanding a cherishing of the wholeness of human personality, the "unmediated wholeness of feeling and thought," and constituting a never-ending challenge to man, emerging from the abyss of meaninglessness and suffering, to be renewed and replenished in the totality of his life.

Justice itself, which has been "in a state of pilgrimage and crucifixion" and now is being slowly liberated from the grip of social and political demonologies in the East as well as in the West, begins to question its own premises. The modern revolutionary movements which have challenged the sacred institutions of society by protecting social injustice in the name of social justice are here examined and re-evaluated.

In the light of this, we have no choice but to admit that the *un*-freedom against which freedom is measured must be retained with it, namely, that the aspect of truth out of which the night view appears to emerge, the darkness of our time, is as little abandonable as is man's subjective advance. Thus the two sources of man's consciousness are inseparable, not as dead but as living and complementary, an aspect of that "principle of complementarity" through which Niels Bohr has sought to unite the quantum and the wave, both of which constitute the very fabric of life's radiant energy.

There is in mankind today a counterforce to the sterility and danger of a quantitative, anonymous mass culture; a new, if sometimes imperceptible, spiritual sense of convergence toward human and world unity on the basis of the sacredness of each human person and respect for the plurality of cultures. There is a growing awareness that equality may not be evaluated in mere numerical terms but is proportionate and analogical in its reality. For when equality is equated with interchangeability, individuality is negated and the human person extinguished.

We stand at the brink of an age of a world in which human life presses forward to actualize new forms. The false separation of man and nature, of time and space, of freedom and security, is acknowledged, and we are faced with a new vision of man in his organic unity and of history offering a richness and diversity of quality and majesty of scope hitherto unprecedented. In relating the accumulated wisdom of man's spirit to the new reality of the World Age, in articulating its thought and belief, *World Perspectives* seeks to encourage a renaissance of hope in society and of pride in man's decision as to what his destiny will be.

World Perspectives is committed to the recognition that all great changes are preceded by a vigorous intellectual re-evaluation and reorganization. Our authors are aware that the sin of *hubris* may be avoided by showing that the creative process itself is not a free activity if by free we mean arbitrary, or unrelated to cosmic law. For the creative process in the human mind, the developmental process in organic nature and the basic laws of the inorganic realm may be but varied expressions of a universal formative process. Thus *World Perspectives* hopes to show that although the present apocalyptic period is one of exceptional tensions, there is also at work an exceptional movement toward a compensating unity which refuses to violate the ultimate moral power at work in the universe, that very power upon which all human effort must at last depend. In this way we may come to understand that there exists an inherent independence of spiritual and mental growth which, though conditioned by circumstances, is never determined by circumstances. In this way the great plethora of human knowledge may be correlated with an insight into the nature of human nature by being attuned to the wide and deep range of human thought and human experience.

In spite of the infinite obligation of men and in spite of their finite power, in spite of the intransigence of nationalisms, and in spite of the homelessness of moral passions rendered ineffectual by the scientific outlook, beneath the apparent turmoil and upheaval of the present, and out of the transformations of this dynamic period with the unfolding of a world-consciousness, the purpose of *World Perspectives* is to help quicken the "unshaken heart of well-rounded truth" and interpret the significant elements of the World Age now taking shape out of the core of that undimmed continuity of the creative process which restores man to mankind while deepening and enhancing his communion with the universe.

RUTH NANDA ANSHEN

Preface

This book is in no sense a comprehensive history of twentieth-century music. It seeks, however, to uncover the springs that have gone to create our music, and assumes that those elements which are most deeply revelatory are probably also the most "valuable." The argument, whatever its anthropological, psychological, philosophical and sociological implications, usually starts from fairly rigorous musical analysis, and some sections can hardly be fully intelligible without reference to the scores discussed. Music quotation, always a clumsy and unsatisfactory aid, seemed inappropriate to a book in a series such as this; I have therefore indicated, where relevant, specified editions, and must hope that readers will make the effort to consult them.

A considerable proportion of the works discussed are theater pieces, or anyway works involving extra-musical elements. This doesn't make the problem of writing about music, in musical terms, any the easier, but it does provide a frame of extra-musical, literary and dramatic reference which may make the argument less difficult to follow, especially for people who have no technical training in music. The choice of theatrical pieces hasn't, I think, involved any distortion of perspective: it's remarkable how much of the finest music of our time seeks to project its aural images into visual and kinetic terms, and this may be another manifestation of our music's derivation from late Wagner, and from *Tristan* in particular.

The germ of the book was a series of lectures which I gave for the Andrew Mellon Trust in the University of Pittsburgh, U.S.A., in 1960. The chapter on New Music in a New World draws on material already published in my book *Music in a New Found Land,*

and is used by kind permission of Barrie and Rockliff, the English publisher, and of Knopf, Inc., the American publisher. The section on Stravinsky's *Oedipus Rex* incorporates material originally published in a symposium on Stravinsky issued by the *Musical Quarterly* and subsequently as a book by W. W. Norton and Co.; acknowledgments are due both to quarterly and publisher. The section on Satie's *Parade* is a rewriting of material published in the Decca Book of Ballet; some of the paragraphs on Britten and Orff originally appeared, in a different form, in the *New Statesman* and the *Musical Times*.

I also owe a debt to many friends and students with whom I have discussed the ideas contained in the book: especially to my friend and pupil Malcolm Troup, from whom I've taken sundry tips that, when his research project is completed, will become part of what promises to be an important book on Messiaen.

W. M.

July, 1966
Department of Music, University of York
England

CALIBAN REBORN

Renewal in Twentieth-Century Music

"this Thing of darkenesse I
Acknowledge mine."

SHAKESPEARE: *The Tempest*

"In that european end meets Ind."

JAMES JOYCE: *Finnegans Wake*

"The artist is always engaged in writing a detailed history of the future because he is the only person aware of the nature of the present."

WYNDHAM LEWIS

I

Revelation and Incarnation: The Legacy of the Past

There is today a widespread belief that music—and the civilization of which music is a part—has reached some kind of crisis. We live, we say, in an age of transition; and while every age is a transition from one era to another, it is true that at some times we are more aware than at others not only of the pace of, but also of the necessity for, change. The awareness of crisis is not, in music, peculiar to our own times; we may point, as parallels, to the end of the fourteenth and the beginning of the seventeenth centuries, and we can learn something from considering in what ways our own crisis resembles, and in what ways it differs from, these earlier crises. There are, however, reasons for believing that the crisis in our own time is more acute than similar crises in Europe's past, if only because the process of change—or our inability to deal psychologically with so much physical change in so short a time—may literally lead to our extinction. The purpose of this book is to consider in what, if any, ways these changes represent a radical departure from Western, European tradition, and if such a departure has occurred, to ask how much or how little it means.

As Europeans, we are all heirs to the Renaissance, that singularly European consciousness of Man's power and glory and, complementarily, of his pathos and frailty. For centuries we have been brought up in the belief that man is, in Sir John Davies' phrase, "a proud and yet a wretched thing," and we have considered art—the creative manifestation of man's potentialities—both as an assertion of our pride and as a confession of our wretchedness. Our art has been concerned essentially with *expression* and with *communication* by way of symbol-making: we have tried to record our responses to the world (which includes other people), and we have wanted to share our responses with our fellow men. In a sense, all our art has been an assertion of our post-Renaissance pride, for it has implied that other people care, or ought to care, about our experience. The post-Renaissance conception of art is basically moral because it assumes that art is concerned with moral responsibilities: to begin with, our own, for we are what we "express," and secondarily, other people's, because they are affected by our expression. This is not the less true when artists have preached, or have pretended to preach, a doctrine of moral irresponsibility, since to ask us to follow the whims of our senses, rather than the demands of Reason or the Will, is still an invitation to act in one way rather than another.

While this conception of art is our birthright and has gone to make the world we live in, we have to realize that in the context of history the notion is both newfangled and restricted. It is relevant to only about the last five hundred years of Europe's history and to the brief life span of her American baby. To this day another and older view of music is prevalent in the East; and this view of music—which we may refer to as Revelation, as opposed to the post-Renaissance doctrine of Incarnation—has by far the longer, if not (for us) the more rewarding, history. Between music as Revelation and music as Incarnation there is one basic technical distinction: music as magic, as contrasted with music as expression, lacks the element of harmony. On the significance of this we shall comment later; for the moment we must inquire into music's nature at its most primitive level. Music can exist—indeed existed for thousands of years—without harmony, but it can hardly exist apart from its two prime constituents, rhythm and melody. If one puts rhythm first, that is because rhythmic significance is possible without melody, whereas melody, being a succession of pitches in time, inevitably implies some kind of rhythmic organization.

What kind of organization is, however, the crucial point. The basic melodic "shapes" are inherent in acoustical facts and in the structure of the human vocal organs. In the music of all primitive cultures, however widely separated in time and place, the natural norm of progression is by the intervals of fifth and fourth, by the *step* which is defined by the difference between fifth and fourth, and by the pentatonic minor third; we find these melodic formulae recurrent in all musically "monodic" cultures, sophisticated and unsophisticated alike. The effect of these melodies will, however, be conditioned by their structure, which in turn is conditioned by two different conceptions of rhythm, one of which we may describe as *corporeal,* the other as *spiritual.* As the term suggests, corporeal rhythm comes from bodily movement: from physical gestures in time, associated with work or play. It thus tends to be *accentual;* the regularity of the stresses measures off Time without necessarily having any relationship to melody. Indeed, accentual rhythm tends to curb melody by reducing it to a short, repeated pattern (in very primitive societies often a mere two-note figure, the pathogenic yell of the falling fourth). The effect of this Time-measuring thus tends to be incantatory and hypnotic. In becoming habituated to Time's beat we cease to be conscious of it, and this unconsciousness of our earth and Time-bound condition is precisely the magic effect that primitive man sought through his music. We can still hear this, today, in a Tahitian drum-accompanied chant, or in the Beatles' beat. The other kind of rhythm, which we have called spiritual, arrives at a similar effect by the opposite means. Whereas corporeal rhythm is accentual, spiritual rhythm is numerical, having the minimal relationship to bodily movement. It thus tends to be subtle and complex in its organization; to suggest, indeed, a self-generative spontaneity that counteracts any sense of periodicity or beat. Whereas corporeal rhythm is divisive or multiplicative (four as a multiple of two two's, two as a division of four), spiritual rhythm is additive (two plus one, plus three, plus five, etc.), and therefore tends to have no regular meter and no strong accents. In effect it is liberative and, therefore, ecstasy-inducing. We shall see later why spiritual rhythm, unlike corporeal rhythm, can flourish only in a monodic music, and can survive only with difficulty, if at all, in a music that is harmonically conceived.

In the music of primitive cultures—and this is true too of the music of children, who are at a primitive stage of evolution—the rhythm is usually corporeal and the music is never self-expression but rather a communal act of work or play which may have magical as well as social significance. But the more developed, the richer a culture becomes—which may or may not mean that it becomes more sophisticated—the more the corporeal rhythm will involve within itself elements of spiritual rhythm. Additive rhythms, often of extreme complexity, may exist over and above the fundamental corporeal rhythm, as in much African music; at a further stage (for instance, in classical Indian music) these complex additive rhythms will be combined with subtle melismatic distortions of pitch in the basically pentatonic patterns of the melody. There is a heterophony of both line and rhythm, whereby the music seems simultaneously rooted to the earth and an escape from it. It is interesting that a similar compromise occurs in European folk music, even in societies whose art-music is unambiguously post-Renaissance in concept. It is, of course, especially noticeable in European cultures that veer toward the East (for instance, the Magyar music that was so richly explored by Bartók), and is a spontaneous part of the folk music of the American Negro, and therefore implicitly of jazz.

As the ancient civilizations grew more complex and less primitive, there was a tendency for corporeal rhythm to be absorbed, or even "sublimated," into spiritual rhythm. This did not affect music alone. East Asian poetry, for instance—that of China, Japan and Mongolia—has no qualitative accents, only quantitative or numerical proportions. Even the dancing has little physical drive. There's a basic two or four pulse which creates an equilibrium—one, two, one, two. But this pulse is so immensely slow that it cannot be apprehended as a beat, and within it the movements of hands, arms and body are infinitely subtle, a manifestation of Being rather than of Becoming, and so beyond temporality. Similarly, the music that accompanies the dancing measures Time in percussive gong tones so slow that they cannot be experienced as meter, while the melodic variations on the basic pentatonic patterns are usually additive in rhythm. This applies even to the music of the Chinese and Japanese theater which, if it is an imitation of human action, is action viewed *sub specie aeternitatis,* to which "development" is extraneous.

In classical Indian music this "spirituality" reaches perhaps its highest point. When the Indian vina player takes up his instrument it is not to "put over" his own personality. The drone, which is eternity, independent and oblivious of our joys or distresses, hums continuously, the music of the spheres. Against it, the player will begin to mull over the raga appropriate to the hour and place. The raga is in no sense the player's invention. It is neither a theme nor a scale, but rather a *series,* an arrangement of pitch relationships which is usually pentatonic at base, though it may introduce chromatic or microtonal intensifications. Almost certainly, the raga's remote origins were in folk song, in the recurrent melodic formulae which the voice employs to "get going," as we can see from the evolution of British or any other folk music. In time, however, these formulae were imbued by centuries of tradition with specific ritualistic or religious associations, which were further sophisticated by the technical refinements of highly skilled virtuosi. Thus the raga became a technical esotericism, and also the Word of God, who has a different word for various times of the day and seasons of the year.

While the vina player tries out the raga appropriate to the time and place, the percussion or tabla player will tentatively explore the tala or rhythmic pattern which is ritualistically relevant. While the tala usually embraces the physical energy of the body, it tends to be an additive pattern, often of considerable complexity; it will increasingly be swept into the melodic player's ecstasy as the "composition" begins. To compose, indeed, is to improvise, with a wealth of microtonal inflection and with the utmost subtlety of rhythmic nuance, on patterns which are preordained. String player and drummer mutually stimulate one another, and it's almost true to say that the composer-player's talent or genius is manifest in inverse proportion to his terrestrial passions, for the better composer he is, the more sensitive to human agony or mirth, the more his improvisation will float and soar, the more his complexities of rhythm will defy the metrical pulse of Time. The fact that he employs pitch distortion—which brings with it a high quota of nervous dissonance—is part of the effect. The anguish and the physical tension of our earthly lives are present (as they are more crudely in the "dirt" of scat singing and jazz horn-playing), and both the distonation and the nasal quality of vocal production are considered to be erotic. Yet the function of the music is precisely to release this tension when the vina player, emulating vocal technique in playing closer and closer to the bridge, achieves his ultimate ecstasy, and his melodic, nonharmonic, nonmetrical music takes flight, liberating both himself and his listener-participants from Time and the Will. It's interesting that jazzmen still use the word "flight" to describe their wilder arabesques; and although these arabesques are cumulative, the sense of progression is irrelevant to them, as it is to those of the Indian vina player. Theoretically, a vina player's (or a jazzman's) inprovisation could go on all day and all night and, to Western ears, sometimes seems to do so, however much we may admire (in both the literal and the colloquial sense) the moments of ecstasy. How irrelevant our temporal and harmonic concepts are to oriental music is indicated by the fact that Indian folk singers can still be heard singing the same tune at and in different times simultaneously, and that Japanese Buddhist monks will sing the same chant in any time and at any pitch (often twenty or more at once) convenient to their voices. In neither case is there any intention to depart from monodic principles, let alone to sing in formal canon or in twenty-part homophony.

It is obvious that to such music the Western theory of communication is not pertinent. There is no audience to be communicated with, for composer-performer and listeners (who will become directly involved in the performer's ecstasy) are participants in a rite. The composer's duty is not to express but to reveal; what he reveals is the Reality within the God-given raga and tala. Such revelation is, however, a human activity, and we may see the "corporeal" and the "spiritual" music as manifestations of complementary aspects of man's nature. Music built upon corporeal rhythm is concerned with man as a social being, engaged in communal activity; music built upon spiritual rhythm deals with Man alone—not with his awareness of his own consciousness, but with his relationship to God. In corporeal music man loses his consciousness of personal identity in equating his lot with that of his fellow beings; in spiritual music he loses this consciousness in discovering, or seeking to discover, the will of God. Some interrelation between the two would seem to be essential for human growth. One reason why the culture of classical Greece has been so important in the history of the human race may be because it came closer than most Eastern cultures to achieving such a dual relationship.

We do not know a great deal about the music of Greek antiquity, but we do know that its melismatic arabesques and additive rhythms were, unlike those of classical Indian music, associated with words. This inevitably entailed more direct "human" references; and we may suspect that corporeal rhythm played a predominant part in the Dionysiac aspects of Greek drama. A Greek tragedy—and for that matter a Greek comedy too—was fundamentally a religious rite; its music seems to have been monodic; and the Greek modes were like ragas in that they had magical properties that were supposed directly to influence human conduct. At the same time it is clear that Greek drama was passionately "humanistic" in a way that a Japanese Noh play was not; and it seems probable that Greek dancing was less static, more accentually percussive, than Indian dance. The balance between the Dionysiac and the Apollonian which the Greeks sought for as an ideal is in one sense an equilibrium between the corporeal and the spiritual. It also, however, brings in another concept which was not to be thoroughly explored, or re-explored, until the Renaissance: for the Apollonian idea involves the subjection of passion by reason, as well as its sublimation into spiritual ecstasy.

This being so, one might have expected that the Greeks, proceeding from the monodic concept, would have gone on to "discover" harmony. Indeed, Pythagorean science *had* discovered it, and was to become the basis of harmonic theory thousands of years later.

Pythagoras, in relating the mathematical laws of Harmonic Proportion to a developed cosmology, had indicated how music could "keep unsteady Nature to her law," as Milton put it; emotional *ekstasis* could be reconciled with the intellectual worship of number, and the claims of body, spirit and intellect be mutually satisfied. What prevented the Greeks from finally achieving this synthesis was in part the qualities to which they owed their greatness. Pre-Socratic Greece was still mainly an oral, nonliterate culture, intuitive, irrational, built on the all-embracing love of the earth goddess, Demeter; its passionate, religious, mystical matriarchy (closer to medieval than to post-Renaissance Europe) remained at war with, and was too powerful to be absorbed by, its new, empirical, rationalistic patriarchy. This *potestas*—this patriarchal authority—was taken over by Roman civilization; in Greece the unity of Pythagorean science split into Platonism and Aristotelianism, and the Dark Ages deliberately separated "spirit" from the physical world. Plato, obsessed with the perfection of circular form, turned his back on reason; Aristotle, cultivating reason, removed it completely from cosmology; and Ptolemy could say that since we can know nothing of the behavior of heavenly bodies precisely because they are heavenly, it is our duty to teach the doctrine of their circular behavior regardless of what may once have been known as scientific fact. Christianity, arising out of the ruin of the ancient world, battened on this separation of spirit from flesh, of belief from reason. St. Augustine counteracted his *omnis natura, in quantum natura, bonum est* with the doctrine of predestination and with the theory that intellectual knowledge was no less a seduction than submission to the flesh. So the Dark Ages reinterpreted cosmology, using the theory of the Chain of Being in a way that has much in common with oriental religions, seeking a ritual protection against sin, guilt and anguish. (See Arthur Koestler, *The Sleepwalkers.*)

Something of this evasion remained when, during the heyday of the Middle Ages, Aristotle was rediscovered and Reason reinstated, as against the Platonic shadow. For Reason was relevant only to man's theological nature, and to his social nature in so far as he lived in a theocratic universe; the wonderful flowering of spirit and, indeed, of humanity must not disturb the status quo or infect a walled-in universe with the blight of mutability—which is still feared, as late as Edmund Spenser. This is why medieval man was so reluctant to investigate the facts of musical harmony, which were part of his theoretical legacy from the ancient world. More than a thousand years later, he still stubbornly turned his back on the implications of Greek theory. It was to take him another two hundred years to admit to the evidence of his ears—and nerves, senses and body. His intellect submitted last.

So the compositional principles inherent in European music before the Renaissance are not radically distinct from those of Oriental music. The music of the Byzantine church may be in direct descent from Greek monody and certainly absorbed elements from oriental cantillation by way of the music of the Jewish synagogue. In Gregorian monody the core of the music is the modal (and basically pentatonic) pattern which, being almost as "natural" as breathing or the heartbeat, becomes (like a raga) a source of creativity. To compose is to extend, embellish, intensify the formula with rich melismata, freely additive in rhythm, culminating in the sequences and tropes which were an ecstatic act of praise. The link with the East is, as we have seen, direct; the composer is always anonymous, and he always starts from the traditional musical "doctrine" of his Church. He does not, like the Indian vina player, re-create the doctrine with each performance; but the traditional forms of the tropes must have been arrived at through a process of improvisatory experiment, and were certainly modified in repetition. The still unresolved arguments as to the correct rhythmic interpretation of plainchant perhaps testify to the fact that the music looks forward as well as back; but we can hardly doubt that the rhythmic conception was in origin numerical, and that if recurrent rhythmic patterns exist, they are not aggressively metrical or Time-dominated. The monks' intention, in singing their chant, must have been very close to the intention of the Indian vina player: by dedication to the Word—his Christianized raga—the plainchanter aimed to liberate the spirit, allowing the melodies to flow, unaccompanied, mainly by step and by pentatonic minor thirds, overriding metrical time and the pull of harmonic tension. He sought freedom from the self through the revelation of the divine; and the nasal quality of his vocal production, reinforced by the church's vaulted echoes, would have had unmistakably Eastern affiliations.

But while medieval performance would certainly have incorporated more "dirt" (in the jazz sense) than do modern attempts to revive or preserve ecclesiastical tradition, it's probably true that Christian chant *denied* more aspects of experience before its sublimatory process could begin. The plainchanter's melismatic tropes and "jubilations," though wilder than anything we're likely to hear in contemporary liturgical performance, were almost certainly less wild than those of his Byzantine and Jewish, let alone his specifically Oriental, forebears; the Christian has become a shade more self-conscious in his yearning for sublimation. This is one way of saying that the Renaissance was latent in Christianity; and in musical terms the change has something to do with the growing importance of words. For while the words in plainchant are impersonal, being *the* Word in a hermetic language different from the normal means of communication, it is significant that European monody preserved its contact with the most "human" of all instruments, the voice; whereas oriental monody, having derived its basic formulae from the voice's spontaneous activity, achieved its highest manifestations in instrumental form.

We can better understand the significance of the affiliation between medieval monody and words if we turn from the doctrinal music of the Church to the secular monody of the Middle Ages—the songs of the troubadours. The nature of the melodic lines in troubadour music is hardly distinguishable from plainchant, for they proceed by step and pentatonic minor thirds, introduce melismatic extensions which are comparable with oriental cantillation, and may even have been directly influenced by Arabian and Moorish music during the Crusades. The correct rhythmic interpretation of troubadour song, even more than of plainchant, is still a matter of scholarly dispute, but it seems highly probable that troubadour singers, being originally their own poets, would have employed flexible additive rhythms derived from their words, and that if the theory of rhythmic proportion is appropriate we should see this not as an aggressive assertion of accentual dance meter, but as a more rudimentary form of the Indian tala. The literary themes of troubadour song center, significantly, on the *sublimation* of terrestrial passion. The Apollonian-Dionysiac relationship of the Greeks is given, in a Christian context, a changed emphasis. The troubadour's Beloved is outside marriage, because marriage is a terrestrial institution; but whether she is the Dark Goddess of Gnosticism or the Virgin Mary or (which is more probable) both at the same time, she is unattainable. Being such, she provokes—especially in the northern, Germanic development of troubadour music—a death wish, inducing an element of melancholy and frustration within the melodies' ecstasy. The essence of plainsong melody is that it seems, in its winging continuity, eternal, whereas the most characteristic and beautiful troubadour melodies counteract their air-borne flow with an obsessive reiteration of falling fourths and fifths. This feature is associated with what may be the tunes' more regularly periodic lilt. In any case the troubadour singer does not invite us to participate in a ritual, as the plainsong cantor does, or as does the Indian vina player, who induces ecstasy (unless, being untalented, he invokes merely boredom). The troubadour singer tells us of his desire and of his sorrow, both unappeased and unappeasable. Though he sings of an eternal longing, for mankind as much as for himself, the Renaissance is already implicit in him. In his melancholy, he says that although the mother of God was a virgin, he cannot but be battered and bruised by his *awareness* of the flesh. Already a dualism is latent: which in musical terms was to lead to the end of the monophonic principle—and of the belief in music as a revelation of the ultimate unity.

The great oriental religions had, of course, always admitted to the eternal dualities of light-dark, hot-cold, self–not self, even the moral issues of good and evil. At the same time they made the evasion of the implications of duality the very heart of their philosophy and ritual: fulfillment could never be through conflict, only through the relinquishing of the Many in the One. Similarly primitive peoples and the members of oriental cultures must have been aware of the simultaneous sounding of tones, without being either philosophically or psychologically interested in exploiting this dualism. Harmony is of its nature a dualistic phenomenon, since it involves two or more tones of different vibration rate, in varying degrees of tension one with another. We know that the troubadours had instruments with which to accompany their monody. We don't know what they did with them, but suspect that they for the most part used instruments merely to double the vocal line, maybe with melismatic embroideries, or to play quasi-oriental drones, or melodic ritornelli between the stanzas. Yet it also seems possible that they—unlike musicians of oriental cultures—may occasionally and fortuitously have explored the effect of simultaneously sounding tones: for they represented a Christian civilization, and Christianity is the one great religion based on *consciousness* of duality. Its God became Man, and in so doing encouraged man to think of his earthly life as drama—a conflict between good and evil. It's probable that Christianity became the dominant creed, surviving through the humanism of the Renaissance and the age of the baroque, precisely because it stressed the fact of human guilt and the possibility of redemption. The Christian symbol, the Cross, is itself a duality, as opposed to the circular eternity symbols of oriental religions.* Even though Christians believed that we live here and now in a vale of tears, they thought that what happened to us in the vale was supremely important, since it affected our chance of future bliss. The idea of life as a pilgrimage itself implies that Time is of consequence, whereas to religions centered on eternity it is irrelevant. This is why the harmonic revolution in European music is inseparable from a revolution in the temporal concept.

One can observe the beginning of this change in the medieval theory of rhythmic proportion itself. Like the Indian talas, the rhythmic "modes" in troubadour song and in medieval music

* Cf. Owen Barfield, *Saving the Appearances:* "The oriental conception of time was essentially cyclic. The picture was of eternal repetition rather than of beginning, progress, and end, and the path of the individual soul to the bosom of eternity was a backward path of extrication from the wheels of desire in which it had allowed itself to become involved. To reach, or to resume, the supreme identity with Brahma, with the Eternal, was the object and its achievement was a matter which lay directly between the individual and the Eternal.

generally had doctrinal and ritualistic significance; the association of "perfect" rhythm (which is triple) with the Trinity dates back at least as far as Philippe de Vitry. Superficially, moreover, this looks like an additive rhythm, two plus one, which is what one would expect of a mystically inclined society. But triple rhythms are also rooted in a fact of nature, for they are the rhythms of breathing (in-hold-out), and thus may have a more direct association with the rhythm of the human voice, and a more immediate relationship to "feeling," than the immeasurably slow duple rhythm of the East. Perhaps it is not an accident that triple rhythms continue to be associated with "human" fulfillment, through the Renaissance and the age of the baroque. Certainly during the Middle Ages the triple additive rhythm is, compared with the Indian talas, so simple that it could also function accentually and corporeally. This *may* have happened in some troubadour monody; it indubitably happened when, in polyphonic music, the triple rhythm had to be to some degree accentual if the performers were to keep together.

The troubadours were not aware of the equivocation at the heart of their music, nor were the creators of harmony aware that they had arrived at a revolutionary principle. Harmony evolved in Europe as a consequence of two accidents that must have occurred in primitive cultures and in the great oriental civilizations also, the difference being that the European Christian was fascinated by the implications of these accidents, whereas the primitive and oriental musicians were not. If one takes part in community singing among untrained voices, one soon becomes aware that, while everyone thinks he or she is singing at the same pitch, some singers adapt the tune to a pitch convenient to their voices; they sing a fifth above or a fourth below the main body of voices without realizing (for the hold of the absolute consonances is so strong) that they are not singing at the same pitch. This is an unconscious example of *organum*, which probably began fortuitously in the medieval Church, but was then deliberately exploited because the sound was awe-inspiring and superhuman, especially when reinforced by the Gothic cathedral's echo. Once the duplication of the voices at different pitches had been admitted, it was only a matter of time before the parts would sometimes move—at first by accident, then by design—in contrary instead of parallel motion. The sound of seconds, thirds and other intervals more sophisticated than fourths and fifths would thus become familiar, and a compositional principle based on the alternation of harmonic tensions would be feasible, if not immediately necessary.

Another accident that occurs in primitive mass singing reinforces this awareness of harmony. The singers, intending to sing the same tune simultaneously, may not succeed; their "wrong notes" will disturb the melodic unison and provide examples of fortuitous harmonization. At first the effects will be chaotic and arbitrary. Before long, however, such heterophonic effects will be used to artistic purpose, and the more skillful singers will be encouraged to embroider melismatic embellishments around the simple form of the melody as sung by the main group. Medieval polyphony sprang from an interaction of these two principles of organum and of melismatic heterophony. Both elements were intended to be an enrichment of traditional monody; neither was meant to be a denial of the monodic principle. Nor was it a denial, at least for a matter of two hundred years. In the polyphony of Perotin the additive triple rhythm often functions corporeally, since a basic 3/8 pulse becomes two measures of 6/8 or four of 12/8 with a pronounced, even dance-like, lilt. But this accentual feeling has, as yet, no harmonic manifestations. The only "real" harmonies are fifths and fourths, passing dissonances being the accidental result of the melismatic elaborations; and the immensely long instrumental notes of the plainsong cantus firmus become the Word, the Rock, upon which the ecstatic melodies proliferate—an effect directly comparable with that of the eternity-drone in Indian music. Despite Perotin's relatively earthly, triple-rhythmed lilt, he dissolves our corporeal energies into spiritual levitation; the whirling of pentatonic figurations around the fundaments of octave, fifth and fourth creates an aural phenomenon close to the tintinabulation of bells. The occasional fortuitous dissonance, evoking unexpected partials, would emphasize this, letting in the "dirt" like the pitch distortion in Indian music: so that although Perotin apparently writes harmonized part-music, its behavior is hardly more harmonic (in the modern sense) than is monophonic oriental chant.

This remains true even as late as Guillaume de Machaut, at the end of the Middle Ages. In rhythms and structure the additive principle still remains dominant. There is a close analogy between the structure of a Machaut motet and that of a Gothic cathedral. The main structure of the cathedral is a feat of mathematical engineering, to which the individual craftsmen add their contributions. Similarly, the medieval motet is built on the rock of the plainsong cantus firmus, the other parts being added separately, each as an independent entity, beautiful in itself, if more beautiful in relationship to the whole. Machaut's famous *Messe de Nostre Dame* is likewise constructed as musical architecture, on linear and metrical-mathematical principles, and his more recognizably melodic form of the cantus firmus—the Word from which the melodic material is derived—has a clear affinity with the "preordained" oriental raga. Similarly the technique of isochronous rhythm—a metrical pattern which remains constant for a given part, though the pitch relationships change—is comparable with the oriental tala, especially since the rhythmic patterns are complex and numerical, and often have doctrinal as well as musical significance. From the harmonic point of view there is more movement and more "density" in Machaut's four-part than in Perotin's three-part texture; nonetheless, the dissonant clashes produced by contrary motion are still not harmony in the post-Renaissance (structural and dramatic) sense. One may compare their effect to that of the gargoyles in a Gothic cathedral. In Machaut's day one entered the church and listened to the music as it was sung and played, as an act of worship. One sought to lose consciousness of personal identity, and while the savage dissonances that intermittently assailed one's ears and the gargoyles that unexpectedly leered down from the walls reminded one of sin and mortality and the nameless horrors that make us human, one no longer needed to fear them. One could forget the gargoyles on the wall and within the mind and senses, as the eyes and soul were swept heavenward by the building's air-borne architecture. Similarly, Machaut's fierce dissonances would be absorbed in the splendor of sonority, the unalterable grandeur of the mathematical proportions, the godlike reiteration of the absolute consonances of fourth and fifth, the ritual tolling of bells and gongs.

It is inevitably difficult for us to respond to this music in a way that is appropriate. For all its sophistication, it has also a Byzantine glory and a quality that is primitively wild and terrifying. Perhaps it has an element of desperation, too: an intuitive awareness that the end of a world is at hand. In the Middle Ages both gargoyles and the creatures of beauty—saints, angels, Mother and Child—that adorn the cathedral are distractions that may be sublimated into the architectural whole. In Machaut's day, however, the process of sublimation had become much more difficult: the gargoyles are more savagely potent, the things of beauty more alluring. There may be a direct manifestation of this desperation in what has been called the restiveness of the late Gothic motet. The desire to impose the ultimate unity on the most intractable experience reaches extravagant lengths. Different texts will be set simultaneously, often in different languages, and although they are usually doctrinally related, the music seems to emphasize rather than to disguise their disparities. The isochronous rhythmic patterns grow so complex that there is no parallel to them until some music of the mid-twentieth century. The patterns are often broken or fragmented by the hoquet or hiccup; even words and syllables are disintegrated, so that their human meaning is unintelligible. Rhythmic contrariety between the parts is carried to fantastic lengths, so that one hardly knows whether the concourse is held together by science, by doctrine or by black magic rather than white. Corporeal rhythm has virtually disappeared; so has the ecstasy induced by spiritual rhythm. Such music is a grotesque perturbation of nature and the end of a world. A new world, and a new principle of order, must grow from an acceptance of human nature—gargoyles and mothers and saints—on its own terms.

This first happened, not unnaturally, in Italy, where late Gothic composers devoted less attention to the rituals of the Church than to the celebration of the world in hunting scenes and nature pieces which were usually a background to sexual love. Here the rhythmic excitations of late Gothic style could find a more spontaneous outlet, and could begin to be combined with triadic harmony of the type which was to lead to harmonic revolution. It was, however, a long time—about a hundred years after Machaut's death—before the implications of the harmonic revolution were fully manifest. Even a very late medieval piece, such as Dunstable's celebrated *Veni Sancte Spiritus,* seems to us to go on "too long," by which judgment we imply the (for us) traditional dichotomy between form and content. The judgment is strictly irrelevant, for although Dunstable was in one sense a man of the Renaissance, his approach to composition remained medieval. He was not concerned with his own response, which had to seek incarnation in Time. He was concerned to create an atmosphere in which, through the medium of his music, an act of revelation could occur. He did not know when, or even if, it would happen, but he did his best to provide the musical circumstances in which it might. Just as an Indian vina player would perform for hours or even, with a few necessary intermissions, all day, while his audience or "participants" came and went, so the ritual music in a medieval cathedral would continue for hours, while the congregation fluctuated.

So the concept of order in Dunstable's *Veni Sancte Spiritus* is unambiguously medieval, linear and mathematical. The plainsong cantus firmus is repeated three times in notational values that decrease "doctrinally" by a third (a musical synonym for the Trinity); the rhythmic structure is isochronous; and there are three doctrinally related texts sung simultaneously. The Christian version of the raga and tala are still present, and the rhythm of the individual lines is still numerical, freely flowing, nonmetrical, dissolving away the sense of temporal progression. The Renaissance element in the music consists in the sensuousness of the triadic harmony, which is mellifluous, even tender, compared with Machaut's Byzantine starkness. But although this sensuousness entails an awareness of the flesh, it does not bring the devil with it. The harmony is not so far from the passive sensuality of the early Renaissance style known as fauxbourdon, wherein the chains of 6:3 triads, floating directionless without a before or after, hypnotize us in sensory delight, like a cat lying on its back, purring in the sun. Dunstable's harmony remains independent of the controlling will, and therefore of temporal progression and of dramatic significance. Nonetheless, that the harmonic principle was admitted meant that sooner or later its implications had to be recognized; and we can almost date a moment in history when this happens. In one of his last compositions—a four-part Ave Regina which he asked to have sung at his deathbed—Guillaume Dufay incorporated an appeal to God to have mercy on His dying Dufay; and this unmedieval intrusion of the personal (we may compare the portraits of the artist or the donor that find their way into Renaissance paintings) provokes too a "modern" harmonic technique. Up to this point the four-voiced music has absorbed its triadic sensuousness into the continuous flow of melody. With the words "miserere tui labentis Dufay," however, the liquid major triad sonorities are abruptly contradicted by a *minor* third; and the dramatic effect of this is inseparable from the fact that it implies opposition, and therefore dualism, rather than monism. Moreover, the effect is inconceivable except in relation to Time. Because it is a shock, we are conscious of *when it happens;* momentarily, the music no longer carries us outside Time but makes us aware that the sands of Time—our time, for we are dying—are running out.

Of course it would not be true to say that "expressive" dissonance had not been used in music before: even in Machaut's Mass the reference to the Crucifixion would seem to have prompted an abnormally virulent coruscation of dissonances. But it might be true to say that *dramatic* dissonance, dependent on the Time sense, had not previously been employed in this way; and that in this passage is implicit the essence of late-Renaissance, sixteenth-century musical technique. In Dufay's music the principle of monism, of oneness, is still present in the survival of cantus firmus technique, and in the imitative principle whereby each part, flowing spontaneously as an act of worship, follows its predecessor. But the music is no longer, like plainsong, an act of worship only; its poly- rather than monophonic principle makes it a social as well as a religious act, and the harmonic order (based on the triad) which the parts now seek is a humanly imposed togetherness. Monody, we have seen, is a matter between man and God. Polyphony may start from the man-God relationship, but inevitably involves social relationships also, since several men attempt to create order out of their separateness, and must modify their separateness accordingly. Then, finally, the dissonant *contrast* in Dufay's setting of the word "miserere" presents us with the element of separateness itself. As soon as we center our experience upon our human identities, in Time, we have to admit that these identities are various and conflicting. The oneness of God is eternal and unalterable, but the oneness that man seeks in his social institutions is fallible, because it must be dependent on the vagaries of individual passion. It is interesting that in medieval polyphony strict imitation was hardly an imperative necessity as an aid to unity between man and God. Once the modern harmonic principle has been admitted, however, polyphonic composers (notably those of the first Netherland school) develop a fanatical obsession with canonic imitation, as a bastion against the terror of duality which their harmony unconsciously expressed. As we shall see, their contrapuntal devices, offsetting the harmonic disintegration of vocal modality, exactly parallel Schoenberg's serial processes, offsetting the harmonic disintegration of diatonic tonality.

Moreover, this harmonic revolution is inseparable from a rhythmic revolution, for as soon as man becomes conscious of his personal identity he can no longer—as could primitive man—achieve a social identity that seems independent of Time. In music, the principle of harmonic order cannot exist without alternations of tension and relaxation such as are not present, to anything like a comparable degree, in a purely monophonic music; and alternation implies progression, a beginning, a middle and an end. Similarly, the concept of the suspended dissonance—the sigh of sorrow, the cry of pain—is inconceivable except in reference to a strong and a weak beat on which the dissonance is prepared and resolved. This is why harmony must imply multiplicative and divisive, not additive, rhythm. Corporeal rhythm has to become at least as important as spiritual rhythm, and to enter into a new relationship with it. We may hope to preserve the integrity of the spirit, but having experienced "the pain of consciousness" we can never again be oblivious of the ticking of Time's clock. The sixteenth century was the great age of clockmaking; all over Europe the tintinabulations of Time's clock now chimed against the tolling bells of worship. Nor is this surprising; for the more *conscious* we are of our humanity, the more sensitive we become to our mortality, which terminates human endeavor.

Sixteenth-century musical technique, then, achieves an equilibrium between vocal melody, dance rhythm and harmonic tension: these elements approximating to the aspects of music as worship, as social function and as personal expression. The balance between these forces is what matters, and sixteenth-century musical theory (significantly owing much to Greek theory) insisted that the health of music depends on the proper interaction of its constituent elements, just as did the health of the body politic. It was not an accident that dance rhythm became, during the Renaissance, a constructive principle in its own right. People have always danced; but in medieval music the dance intrudes into "serious" music (which was usually liturgical) as a science or magic of numbers rather than as physical and sensual impulse, and we have seen that in this respect the Middle Ages have something in common with oriental cultures. In the sixteenth century, however, dance became a constructive principle in its own right, closely related to harmonic order: and almost a substitute for a religious principle. The order of human institutions as manifested in the ritual of the dance ought to be a simulacrum of the divine order. This is why the Civil Music and the Divine Music had to be complementary, which (as we have seen) they strictly were in terms of musical technique. The "divine" freedom of vocal polyphony (spiritual rhythm) was now in part ordered by the "human" principle of dance movement and of harmonic solidarity. Conversely, the human order of dance music and of madrigalian homophony (corporeal rhythm) never completely lost contact with the divine order of vocal counterpoint.

The truly revolutionary element in sixteenth-century technique was, however, the third element: that of harmonic tension, as a manifestation of personal passion. The realities of passion could hardly be evaded in an art based on a humanly oriented society; yet the preoccupation with dissonance was always liable—as was evident even as early as Dufay's "miserere"—to threaten the dance-dominated social order. Renaissance men believed that it was precisely as a resolver of the dichotomy between the Many and the One that the traditional, divine associations of music could be most important. This may explain the almost obsessive influence exerted by the Orphean myth during the sixteenth century. The new music —*musica humana*—could express the realities of man's passion. But the process of self-discovery ought also to be a revelation of man's divine origin; *musica humana* ought also to put man in touch with the other music, *musica mundana,* the music of the spheres. So Man-Orpheus may become, through the joy and the suffering his music represents, a thing of wonder who may move the gods to pity and succor him. In so far as this happens, man becomes himself godlike. Though his music is still a ritual act, it is now not so much an act of revelation as an act of incarnation. This is what Monteverdi's *Orfeo*—the first artistically significant opera—is about.

Throughout Shakespeare's plays music is valued as a manifestation of human passion, as when Mariana at the Moated Grange uses the boy's song as a means of assuaging her frustrated passion. But the point lies in the assuagement: the *musica humana* puts her in touch with the *musica mundana,* which helps her to go on living. Similarly, Lear's "restoration" music is passion music in every sense: a string fancy which starts from human passion yet dissolves its (harmonic) suffering in the benediction of quasi-vocal polyphony. The act of incarnation may lead to revelation: the Flesh become Word, and the Word Flesh. Like sixteenth-century technique itself, this was an equivocation which, in spite or because of its richness, could not be long maintained. Shakespeare and Byrd could have occurred only at this time, when an extraordinarily potent apprehension of human sensuality and mortality could be reconciled with an awareness of divine grace. Yet some such equivocation remained an ideal even when Europe had abandoned the equivocation and come down heavily on the side of the flesh: and this may be why, during the seventeenth century, a pronounced elegiac tone enters

To his celestial consort us unite,
To live with him, and sing in endles morn of light.

The lingering, protracted rhythm of the final line reinforces the wistfulness inherent in the passage, and the wistfulness remains, whether we think of the lines in personal terms (we will be fulfilled only when we are dead), or whether we think of them as a prophecy about the destiny of the human race. The whole of Milton's work proves that he knew that, if ever the prophecy were fulfilled, it could not be in the form of a return to the past, since innocence once lost is lost forever.

Milton's image of light is employed in a then obsolete, almost medieval sense. The essence of the "pierced" technique in Gothic architecture—or of the art of medieval illumination, or even of the texture of Gothic polyphony—was that it let light *through,* being an act of revelation: whereas men of the post-Renaissance world were interested in shedding light *on* the variety of the visible and tactile universe. The discovery of visual perspective, which directly parallels the discovery of harmonic depth in music, began as a desire for verisimilitude, a literal imitation of the external world. Soon it became inseparably related to the need for information; interlocking together, "An exactly repeatable pictorial statement, a logical grammar for the representation of space relationship in pictorial statements, and the concepts of relativity and continuity revolutionized both the descriptive sciences and the mathematics on which the science of physics rests."* For medieval man neither space nor time was homogeneous, and medieval painters often repeated a single figure many times in the same picture, since they were interested in the connected meanings of various possible relationships rather than in the logic of geometric optics. On the other hand, the geometric space invented in classical antiquity and rediscovered at the Renaissance could be cut and parceled up in any direction; and this is connected with a Rabelais's desire to *conquer* the world of gigantically inflated physical appetites, with the "hypnotic immoderate thirst after humane learning" referred to by Donne, with the

* William Ivins, *Prints and Visual Communication.*

more trivial itemizing of the Renaissance (as represented by Jonson's Sir Politick Would-Be) and in general with the splintering of social activity and of the private life of the senses into specialized segments. Marshall McLuhan has suggested that in *King Lear* Shakespeare offers us something like a medieval sermon-exemplum "to display the madness and misery of the new Renaissance life of action," the "frenzy to discover a new over-all interplay of forces."

The musical parallel to these disintegrative and reintegrative forces was, we have seen, the phenomenon of harmony. Harmony is of its nature a duality, since it involves more than one tone in shifting vibration ratios, which in turn produce alternating degrees of tension. Sixteenth-century theory and practice had managed to preserve an equilibrium between the human and the divine; but it was inevitable that in time the "pain of consciousness"—which in music involves the awareness of harmonic contrariety—should destroy the old order. This is evident by the early seventeenth century, when disruptive dissonance has enfeebled both vocal modality and polyphonic unity, and when Monteverdi's Orphean opera has given a mythological parallel to what was already implicit in his madrigals. The new order that was emerging negates Milton's view of the purpose of art as revelation, and it is not an accident that this second great revolution in musical history exactly complements the final acceptance of the Copernican system, which was unequivocal by about 1600. For as long as the earth was considered to be the center of a divinely appointed universe, the relationship between Man and Divinity could remain intimate. When once, however, the First Cause was shifted from the periphery of the universe into the physical body of the sun, from which all things derived life, man's relationship to God became too complex to be apprehensible. It seemed easier, as well as more logical, to dismiss God as a mystical entity; to concentrate instead on man's ability, through his intellect, to explain away the mathematical processes of nature (seeing God as geometry) and at the same time to rejoice in man's power to appreciate, understand, and therefore control his sensual passions. During the course of the seventeenth century we can observe how man attempted, in his art forms, to discover means of ordering the human passions which Renaissance consciousness had released. If any extra-human sanction was given to them, it was usually by analogy with the mathematical or scientific "laws" of the natural world—the gravitational pulls of Newtonian physics. The important point, however, is the manner in which natural law is used as an analogy for human, social institutions, so that the world power of the God-King comes to take the place of the divine power of God.

This is evident in Dryden's St. Cecilian odes, which, written only about forty years later than Milton's *At a Solemn Musick,* are as "modern" as Milton's poem was outmoded. He begins by relating music not to the divine order, but to the mechanical view of Nature:

> From Harmony, from Heav'nly Harmony
> This Universal Frame began:
> When Nature underneath a heap
> Of jarring Atoms lay,
> And could not heave her Head,
> The tuneful Voice was heard from high:
> "Arise, ye more than dead."
> Then cold, and hot, and moist, and dry,
> In order to their stations leap,
> And Musick's pow'r obey.

The "force" may be called heavenly in that it is the First Cause, but once the jarring atoms have cohered to create the Newtonian universe, music's power is to be valued only for its human effects. These are twofold. Music's order is a social analogy, for the disruptive tensions of harmony must bow to the public ceremonial of the dance and to the scheme of tonality which was closely related to divisive dance rhythm—just as the individual must be subservient to the state. But music's function is Orphic too, and a properly ordered Whole leads to the fullest expression of the Parts. Thus music is to be valued for its direct effect on human conduct. The trumpet's loud clangor excites us to arms, the double double beat of the thundering drum makes us yet more bellicose, the warbling flute renders us more amorous, and so on. Indeed, the universal order is dedicated only to the fulfillment of man's sensual nature. Though "from Heav'nly Harmony/This Universal Frame began," it runs through "all the compass of the Notes" in order that the Diapason may "close full in Man." Milton deplores the loss of the "perfect Diapason," the octave that was man's oneness with God; for Dryden, the octave is synonymous with Man himself, who is thus the apex of creation. Through the enjoyment of his senses, the command of his reason, and his power over Nature, man has taken God's place. This is the fulfillment of the Renaissance's sensual-material ostentation, which had in turn been made possible only by the economic development of a mercantile society. The Renaissance had, indeed, directly symbolized the deification of man in the ceremony of the King's Two Bodies—his real, mortal body which was carried, at his funeral, to its last resting place and to dusty disintegration; and his garishly colored effigy, made of relatively durable *material,* which represented his "eternal" divinity as a terrestrial institution.

It is not therefore surprising that the divine or mystical aspects of music, associated with St. Cecilia and with the organ, are mentioned in Dryden's poem only perfunctorily, among the other affective attributes of music: having a beatific vision is one among the many varieties of experience, like making love or enjoying a good dinner. Orpheus, Dryden says, could transport savages, and even trees, into a state of ecstasy; complementarily, Cecilia can make angels mistake earth for heaven. This was precisely what men of the heroic world wished to do: to believe so potently in man's glory that they could imagine that paradise on earth was feasible. Dryden's longer St. Cecilian ode, *Alexander's Feast,* explicitly presents the God-King of classical antiquity as symbol of Modern Man. He has his lovely Thais by his side, "like a blooming Eastern Bride," and—with the help of the music of Timotheus, here equated with Orpheus—he fulfills his sensuality, as well as his sexuality, exhibiting his heroic stature by loving more, drinking more, fighting more, weeping more than any ordinary mortal. Significantly, it was during the sixteenth and cumulatively the seventeenth century that sex became supremely important in European culture. In primitive musics the complexities of percussive rhythm transform the erotic in our natures into something approaching religious ecstasy; even in classical Indian music the erotic is still manifest in the drumming, though it is an encouragement rather than an embarrassment to the "spiritual" proliferation of melody. Only in Christian chant and polyphony does there develop a dichotomy between sexual and spiritual impulse, related to the dualism of harmony; only in baroque art does this dichotomy become a primary impetus to creation. In a humanistically oriented world we are *aware of* sex (the basic human instinct from which, indeed, life starts) as a fundamental human division and conflict; yet we may find in it a substitute for religious experience, in the sense that duality may seem to be momentarily obliterated in a Time-denying act of physical union.

So in Dryden's poem music is synonymous with the fulfillment of the sensual appetites. Through it, Alexander's ears may be (in appropriately sexual metaphor) ravished, after which he—human though he is—"Assumes the God,/Affects to Nod," and even "seems to shake the spheares." Once more, Cecilia is brought in only at the end, somewhat apologetically. She shares the crown with Timotheus (equated with Orpheus), because he "rais'd a mortal to the skies;/She drew an angel down." We are left in no doubt that Timotheus's achievement is considered more impressive. If there is a kind of stupidity in this assumption, there is also tremendous courage. This comes out in the epilogic stanza to the earlier St. Cecilian ode:

> As from the pow'r of Sacred Lays
>   The Spheres began to move,
> And sung the great Creator's praise
>   To all the bless'd above;
> So, when the last and dreadful hour
> This crumbling Pageant shall devour,
> The TRUMPET shall be heard on high,
> The Dead shall live, the Living die,
> And Musick shall untune the Sky.

So at the end the Trumpet no longer excites to vainglorious expressions of a power that is in the last resort self-love; becoming the last trump, it tells us that we are snuffed out like a candle. Music inverts its traditional function, as John Hollander has pointed out; instead of reminding us of the divine purpose, it "untunes" heaven itself. Mundane music, in the modern sense, has defeated *musica mundana.*

This inversion precisely complements the latter end of the ancient world. Greek civilization merged into Roman civilization, and that into the Dark Ages, because its mysticism could not ultimately absorb the implications of rationality, literacy and technology; complementarily, at the turn into the eighteenth century Europe's materialism rejected spirit. Either way, Reason is divorced from Belief, and the Pythagorean harmony relinquished. In the light of this we can understand why all baroque music, from Monteverdi to Handel, is a celebration of man's humanity and at the same time a paradox. It attempts to impose the unity of (corporeal) dance rhythm on the chaos of man's harmonic passions; and the additive rhythm of speech inflection, now represented not by liturgical chant but by operatic recitative, gets progressively less significant musically, as the dance-dominated aria grows stronger. But a humanly imposed order can never be finally satisfying, because man, not being in fact god, is both fallible and mortal. This is what all the great operatic myths of the period are "about"; in the old sense of the term there is no spiritual music in the baroque era, no music conceived as an act of revelation. All the greatest music of the seventeenth century *yearns* for the lost unity: this is why Monteverdi's and Purcell's ariosi are poised so poignantly between corporeal and spiritual rhythm; why Purcell was obsessed, even more than men of the sixteenth century had been, with the dualistic pain of false relation; and why the elegiac flavor of Purcell's finest music comes from an intuitive recognition of the conflict between the new and the old values, exactly parallel to that expressed in Milton's poem. Similarly, if Bach is, for us, the greatest of all "religious" composers that is because his music reconciles the greatest awareness of a spiritual order (not unrelated to Pythagorean number symbolism) with the maximum awareness of "the pain of consciousness": the most "perfect" development of contrapuntal science and linear growth (often overriding, even contradicting, the metrical pulse) with the highest density of harmonic tension.

Bach, in achieving so sublime a fusion of the divisive and the additive, the corporeal and the spiritual, is of course exceptional in his period. Yet paradox is inherent in the central convention of the classical baroque; for while the *aria da capo* is a static, non-developing form which "gets nowhere," since the recapitulation is identical with the exposition except for the additional ornamentation, the mere fact that there is a "middle section" admits to the possibility of dualism. The middle section may habitually serve an architectural rather than a dramatic function, but it was not there by chance, and being there, must inevitably be used, sooner or later, for contrast rather than balance. The central theme of heroic opera is the failure of heroism: the ultimate impossibility of man's "assuming the god." So man gave up the attempt. Admitting to a duality between the Self and the World, he came to see that this duality concerned every man; not merely our leaders, who are fallible as we are, but every one of us, in so far as we are human. A humanistic philosophy must lead to what we now call democracy; for if one submits to no law except that which is man-made, the question will soon be asked, Why *that* man (Louis XIV or whomever) rather than another, rather than *me?* If everyone wants to be his own master, he becomes responsible for his own destiny, and he must understand his own nature before he can hope to influence other people.

So there is a change, within the conventions of art, from an "objective" to a more "subjective" approach. *Opera seria,* in the heroic age, was objective in that it was an imitation of men in action. Their behavior was, of course, inseparable from the imaginative life of the man who created them, but it was a projection of that inner life, having direct reference to the behavior of the public that participated in it. When music lost its public significance as a ritual of humanism, it became "public" only in the sense of being entertainment; much rococo music was the relatively plain man's music of social persiflage, an agreeable noise to eat or chatter to. The imaginative meanings of music turned inwards; and the central convention of the age of democracy—the sonata—became, in the hands of Haydn, Mozart and particularly Beethoven, a subjective expression of a dualism within the mind. For Beethoven, the gargoyles within cannot be sublimated in a ritual act, as they were in the Gothic cathedral, nor can they be brushed aside, as they sometimes were in the anti-masques of heroic opera. The battle has to be fought out and the victory won within the "Becoming" which is Beethoven's sonatas and symphonies. Beethoven's triumph of the will is humanism's supreme achievement, and in triumphing Beethoven destroys the barrier between the "inner" and the "outer" life. Ego-assertion could hardly go further than Beethoven carries it in his middle period works, in which the desire to reconcile the "separateness" of harmonic contrariety with the "togetherness" of corporeal rhythm attains a violence that is not far from frenzy. Yet at the height of this frenzy Beethoven spoke of his art to Bettina Brentano in the following terms: *

This is harmony, this is expressed in my symphonies in which the confluence of many-sided forms surges along in one bed to its destination. In them, one can feel that something eternal, infinite, never wholly comprehensible, is contained in every product of the human spirit, and although my works always give me a sense of having succeeded, I feel an insatiable hunger to recommence like a child—even though the last work seemed to have been exhausted with the last beat of the kettle-drum which inculcated my joy and my musical convictions upon the audience. (Speak to Goethe about this, tell him to listen to my symphonies, for then he will admit that music is the only entrance to the higher world of knowledge which, though it embraces me, a man cannot grasp.) A rhythm of the spirit is needed in order to grasp the essence of music: for music grants us presentiments, inspiration of celestial sciences, and that part of it which the mind grasps through the senses is the embodiment of mental cognition. Although minds live on it, as we live on air, it is still a different thing to be able to grasp it intellectually. Yet the more the soul takes its

* Translated by Michael Hamburger in *Beethoven: Letters, Journals and Conversations* (London, 1951). Bettina Brentano is usually considered a romantically unreliable authority; this conversation sounds convincing, however—certainly more Beethovenian than Bettinian.

sensuous nourishment from music, the more prepared does the mind grow for a happy understanding with it. Yet few ever attain this stage; for just as thousands marry for love and love is never manifested in these thousands, although they all practice the craft of love, so thousands have intercourse with music and never see it manifested. Like all the arts, music is founded upon the exalted symbols of the moral sense: all true invention is a moral progress. To submit to these inscrutable laws, and by means of these laws to tame and guide one's own mind, so that the manifestations of art may pour out: this is the isolating principle of art. To be dissolved in its manifestations, this is our dedication to the divine which calmly exercises its power over the raging of the untamed elements and so lends to the imagination its highest effectiveness. So always art represents the divine, and the relationship of men towards art is religion: what we obtain from art comes from God, is divine inspiration which appoints an aim for human faculties, which aim we can attain.

We do not know what it is that grants us knowledge. The grain of seed, tightly sealed as it is, needs the damp, electric warm soil in order to sprout, to think, to express itself. Music is the electric soil in which the spirit thinks, lives and invents. Philosophy is a striking of music's electric spirit; its indigence, which desires to found everything upon a single principle, is relieved by music. Although the spirit has no power over that which it creates through music, it is yet joyful in the act of creation. Thus every genuine product of art is independent, more powerful than the artist himself, and returns to the divine when achieved, connected with men only in as much as it bears witness to the divine of which they are the medium. Music relates the spirit to harmony. An isolated thought yet feels related to all things that are of the mind: likewise every thought in music is intimately, indivisibly related to the whole of harmony, which is oneness. All that is electrical stimulates the mind to musical, flowing, surging creation. I am electrical by nature.

Is it not extraordinary that Beethoven who, in the ego-dominated, Time-obsessed finale of the *Seventh Symphony,* created music which would seem to be the polar opposite to oriental monody or Christian plainchant, should thus express belief in the pre-Renaissance doctrine of music as revelation? He stresses music's humanistic efficacy: it "tames and guides" the passions and in so doing establishes our moral identities. But it does this, not through an assertion of the Will, but through submission. In so far as this submission is to God as absolute, it might seem that Beethoven is merely denying Europe's history and his own transcendent contributions to it. But he is not saying that for him art could or should be pure monism, like plainchant; he is rather saying that if, like the oriental or medieval monodist, he must perform an act of sublimation he, as a post-Renaissance man, can do this only by accepting the senses' terrors and the mind's contradictions as part of the pattern of the whole. This, indeed, is what he came to do in his "third period" works; and in this respect his account of his art is both Jungian and Freudian, while his use of the term "electrical" anticipates some very recent theories about the nature of the human mind. There is something awe-inspiring in the fact that Beethoven, employing a key word of his time that was then but obscurely understood, should prophetically have hinted at truths we are just beginning to apprehend. For him the monism of monody would have been "indigent," like philosophy. His sublimation is born of the pain of consciousness, as is manifest in the techniques of the music of his last years.

The dualities that began to appear in European music at the Renaissance—those between harmony and counterpoint, subject and countersubject, polyphony and homophony, tonic and dominant, content and form, and so on—prove to be musical synonyms for wider and deeper dichotomies between thought and feeling, extroversion and introversion, individual and state, art and science. The separation of the functions—what Blake called "the spectre of the Reasoning Power in Man . . . separated from Imagination and enclosing itself as in steel"—can reduce us to submission to Macbeth's "Tomorrow and tomorrow and tomorrow"; and in so far as Cartesian separation—"single vision and Newton's sleep"—may turn knowledge into a mere mode of sequence, nothing can assure us of one instant's being continued into another. Descartes called this the terror of failure in Time. We have seen that it dominates, or threatens to dominate, Beethoven's *Seventh Symphony:* but it proved to be a prelude to works wherein divisions are healed through a return to springs of the unconscious life. Perhaps it is not altogether fanciful to hold, with Marshall McLuhan, that some such intuitive search for a new-old organic "wholeness" may (to pick up Beethoven's own analogy) in fact have hastened the discovery of electromagnetic waves. In any case, no later artist could be oblivious of Beethoven's confrontation of modern man's predicament. Wagner may have been wrong in regarding himself as Beethoven's direct successor, and we would not immediately think of him as a religious composer in the sense that Beethoven was in his last years. Nonetheless, Wagner too had to roll back all aspects of experience into the unconscious, obliterating traditional distinctions between the outer and the inner life, and his life's work also culminated in a mystical act. *Tristan und Isolde* is the end of a phase in human consciousness which began with the Renaissance; it is also, we are often told, the beginning of modern music. We shall therefore start our inquiry into the nature of the twentieth-century revolution, if that is what it is, with a consideration of some aspects of *Tristan,* and of certain works of Schoenberg, regarded as sequels to the Wagnerian cycle.

II

Eros and Agape: A Theme in Wagner, Schoenberg and Webern

Wagner was an opera composer, not a composer of instrumental sonatas; yet for him opera had become, by the last years of his life, no longer a public or a social event. Indeed, he spent much of his life attacking conventional opera—which had been in origin and history a social ritual of humanism—as a sham, while advocating his own form of music-drama that had many of the characteristics of a religion. Bayreuth was the temple for the worshipers to congregate in; what they celebrated was the projection of Wagner's own inner life as a "modern myth." It is significant that Wagner, representing humanism's ultimate climacteric, should have deified the ego in its most fundamental impulse, that of sex. Whereas Beethoven, in his last works, appeased the anguish of sonata-conflict in the oneness of fugue and the continuity of song-variation, Wagner started, more primitively, from the most fundamental reality known to him: the surge of harmonic tensions which was his own erotic life. From them he derived, in his later work, a polyphonic-harmonic texture which became a cosmos. There is some evidence to suggest that Wagner was aware of what we would call both the Freudian and the Jungian implications of his operas; certainly he thought of himself as "standing for" humanity (as Christ had once done!), and could say, with sublime self-confidence, that the building of Bayreuth was the fulfillment of the destiny which he had planned for himself and humanity.

It is well known that *Tristan und Isolde* is in one sense a dramatization of the situation existing in Wagner's life at the time, in the triangular relationship between himself and Otto and Mathilde Wesendonck. More significant, however, is the fact that in this most directly autobiographical of his works, Wagner should have chosen to re-create the Tristan legend; for of all the great medieval stories, that of Tristan most potently expresses man's awareness of Eros, a simultaneous longing for the senses' fulfillment and for their extinction. At the end of the cycle that began with the Renaissance, Wagner takes up this theme and imbues it, in his fervid, passion-laden chromatic harmony, with five hundred years' burden of consciousness, sensuality, frustrated aspiration, and guilt: with the awareness that we have seen to be latent in troubadour song, though it could not then be expressed. The opera begins with a marvelous musical image for this burden of sensuality, aspiration, and guilt: for the notorious "Tristan chords" consist of interlocked perfect and imperfect fourths. Now in the Middle Ages the perfect fourth and its inversion, the perfect fifth, had been the musical synonym for God, the Absolute Consonance according to Pythagorean science, whereas the imperfect fourth or fifth—the tritone—was the Devil ("Si contra fa diabolus est"). The genesis of the opera is thus the most fundamental dualism, which since the Fall is inherent in sexuality itself; in this sense the four and a half hours of the opera are a protracted attempt at an orgasm which would resolve the dichotomy between spirit and flesh. This is implicit in the nature of the Wagnerian sequence, which is a musical symbol for the interdependence of life-instinct and death-instinct. The rising sixth and falling chromatic scale with which the Prelude opens is repeated sequentially over and over again. It urges the music forward, especially since the sequences usually rise; yet at the same time each sequence is also a cessation, a failure, in so far as it falls back to the point it started from, to try again. From the anguish of the rising-falling phrase, the repeated sequences, the drooping appoggiaturas and the tense dissonance, proliferate the themes and motives of the entire, gigantic score in what Wagner positively, if wistfully, called "endless melody." Only at the very end is the frustrated aspiration resolved.

Most significant is the manner of this resolution. From the literary-dramatic aspect, Wagner's adaptation of the Tristan myth is designed to show in three stages (or acts) how the only fulfillment is that of personal passion; how this cannot be achieved except by separation from the conditions of the material world (society, civilization, domestic loyalties); and finally, how it cannot be achieved within Time at all. And in a sense, as Mr. Joseph Kerman has ably demonstrated, the end is implicit in the beginning. In the first act it is the fact that the lovers believe that they have accidentally drunken Death (the love-potion) that releases their passion and frees them from conventional restraints. The second act shows that failure to live out their love in the world; and the climax, when Melot stabs Tristan, or rather Tristan wounds himself on Melot's sword, is the consequence of the inner conflict generated by the attempt at compromise. It creates what we would call nervous breakdown, and it is from his state of near-paralysis that Tristan hears, at the beginning of Act III, the Shepherd's pipe, which (as represented by cor anglais) sounds like an infinitely forlorn, broken, instable vision of Paradise lost. At what may be the beginning of the end of the harmonic cycle in European music, Tristan—or Wagner—hears, emerging out of the deepest, darkest, weariest permutation of the Tristan chords and motive, *a continuously monophonic, unaccompanied line*. Moreover, the nature of this unaccompanied melody is profoundly interesting: for it is a *linear* version of the perfect and imperfect fourths and fifths of the Tristan chords themselves. It starts from the perfect fifth, which is God, but then crumbles into imperfect fifths and fourths, wandering chromatically in long, nonmetrical convolutions, seeking but only intermittently finding again the fifth's perfection. Both the fluid, noncorporeal rhythm and the chromatically intensified melismata have an oriental flavor, and invoke the spirit of troubadour monody, though the innate melancholy of troubadour music is, of course, deepened by centuries of harmonic "consciousness."

Once Tristan has heard, however faintly, the Shepherd's monody, the process of regeneration may begin, not merely for him, but for post-Renaissance man. In this last act of *Tristan* Wagner does what had long been latent in his operatic technique, for the action is traumatic and, with the possible exception of the arrival of Mark, takes place entirely within Tristan's mind. As Kerman has pointed out, it deals with what one can accurately term Freudian regeneration. The reminiscence of monodic innocence induces Tristan, from near-death, to yearn for "day," but the resurgence of harmonic passion produces in him only agony, for the pain of living is too much to be borne. So he curses Day, which is life; and his ecstasy of anticipation, when Kurwenal leads him to expect Isolde's coming, subsides in another enormous frustrated cadence. At this point the monodic piping is the *empty* sea: the unknown and the unconscious, to which Tristan must surrender. It is this surrender which is effected in Tristan's immense monologue, which this time is distantly accompanied by the piping: so that although the process of curse and relapse is repeated, it is also changed. Now the piping leads Tristan away from amnesia toward an acceptance of his and our pain. He re-experiences the events of his traumatic past: not merely the events of the opera, but also those of his childhood and even the life and death of his father and mother. The gigantic recapitulation of the events of the first act is both a musical and an experiential resolution: an act of understanding and, indeed, of revelation. So the last curse becomes the purgation of his own guilt; it was *I myself* who brewed the potion, and man is responsible only to himself. But this ultimate climax to humanism is also an admission of humanism's inadequacy, for the revelation is also an initiation. Isolde at last comes, Tristan revives in a state beyond Day or curse or yearning, and the Shepherd pipes his "new tune," from which the chromatic anguish has been purged away, so that it is innocently diatonic, even pentatonic.

Seventeenth-century humanism, we saw, had thought of the sexual act as a dying, which seemed to negate Time. Now the admission is overt; the only escape from duality is in death itself, and Tristan dies to the merging of the Love and Death themes, which are now one. The ultimate beatitude is left to Isolde, as the orchestra at very long last resolves the tritonal tension of the Tristan chords into a luminous B major triad, infinitely sustained—infinitely in the sense that whenever the chord fades to silence must seem too soon. By this time the lovers are no longer separate beings. They are the male and female principle within Wagner himself, and within us all; and Wagner gives to the female the heavenly gift of intuition. At the end, Isolde is pure *anima,* into which *animus* is both absorbed and absolved.

Like Beethoven's last piano sonatas and quartets, Wagner's *Tristan* thus expresses the end and the inversion of humanism. The distinction between them lies in the fact that Beethoven entered his paradise in the sublime melodic proliferations of the arietta of Opus 111, whereas Wagner, performing a mystical act in dissolving time, consciousness and sexuality, does not completely achieve this lyrical consummation. The Shepherd's pentatonic "new tune" is notably inferior to his original melody, which was still tremulous with chromatic yearning, whereas the new tune of Beethoven's arietta might be called the fulfillment of his life's work. But it is given to few to enter paradise, which may be why Beethoven's last works had no direct successors, while Wagner's last works were the beginning of modern music. The greatness of *Tristan* is that although it tells us that perfect love can be realized only in nirvana, it affirms and reaffirms the nobility of man's aspiration. This too is the burden of the subjective mythological cycle of *The Ring*. By the time we reach *Die Götterdämmerung* the Dark Forest is unequivocally the Artist-Hero's mind, and although Brünnhilde is still the white dove, the troubadour's Eternal Beloved to be won or lost, the dark and light forces that fight for her are inextricably mingled, being aspects of one consciousness. This is why Hagen has such uncanny potency, and why Siegfried becomes his own betrayer. There can be no simple social answer to so cataclysmic an upheaval, no canalizing of harmonic tension by jolly fugato, or by the public conventions of aria or dance. All these external symbols of the things that make humanism workable have vanished; there *is* no fugato, no aria, no dance, only the surge of the symphonic texture which must work out the motives' musical and experiential destiny

—and has been doing so, not merely (as in *Tristan*) over four and a half hours, but through four enormous operas. One may feel claustrophobia—and rebellion—in submitting so utterly and for so long to Wagner's consciousness, yet one has no choice in the matter. And what makes one finally submit is that *The Ring's* ego-assertion has the "terrifying honesty" of great art. For Wagner's gods are men, or Man as he might be if all men could be Wagner; yet the cycle concludes with the man-god's twilight. Man relinquishes his attempt to be totally responsible for his destiny; Valhalla perishes in the purgatorial fire and—like the Wagnerian sequence itself—returns to its source, being renewed in the waters of the unconscious.

This return to the springs of consciousness—almost to pre-consciousness—has bearing on the distinction between *Tristan* and Wagner's last opera, *Parsifal,* which is also *Tristan's* imaginative complement. For the dark brother—the Hagen figure—is virtually banished, or reduced, in Klingsor, to impotence: while the heroic ego—the Siegfried figure—is transformed into Parsifal's pity for "the wound of the world." This could not have happened without a Christian heritage, but is not necessarily a Christian theme: what happens is that the burden of consciousness—the agony of yearning that had made Tristan and Isolde quintessentially human—is released, along with the fevered chromaticism; and in the vastly slow exfolitation of harmonic polyphony time (as Gurnemanz put it to Parsifal) is one with space. In a sense one might say that the immense slowness of the harmonic pulse of *Parsifal* is Wagner's most "prophetic" achievement—more so than the chromaticism of *Tristan.* It's a renunciation of the basic principle of opera which, having begun as the central expression of European humanism, had always been concerned with the dominance of the will. Parsifal uncovers the path through the Dark Forest: which Debussy and Schoenberg, and ultimately Boulez, had to take.

After Wagner, submission to the dark forest or to the waters of the unconscious becomes an obsessive theme. It may, of course, be negative, a search for oblivion. In the music of Delius, for instance, the burden of the passion-laden, Wagnerian appoggiatura is again too great to be borne, and the ego longs to lose itself in "innocent" pentatonic arabesque and in the eternal nonhumanity of sea and hills. Out of the tension of chromatic harmony flows a new kind of harmonically born polyphony which, especially in the choric vocal writing, wings and sings. Yet the contrast between the chromaticism of the harmony and the pentatonic tendency of the melody produces, in Delius's most characteristic music, the pronouncedly nostalgic flavor which differentiates it from Wagner: it longs for a lost Eden, not for a Paradise regained. This is obvious if one considers Delius's opera *A Village Romeo and Juliet* as a sequel to Wagner's *Tristan und Isolde*. The theme is the same, for the opera deals with the impossibility of achieving an identity between Word and Flesh, between spirit and body, in the conditions of the temporal world. The difference is that the lovers are young; we first meet them as children, and they remain childlike, at the dawn of consciousness, when they grow up to sing their love-music. What destroys them is a sordid squabble over material possessions; love and property, which are the conditions of this life, cannot mix. But their answer to this situation is not, like that of Tristan and Isolde, to try to grow up; it is rather to wish they were children again, preconscious. This probably explains the ambiguous effect of the Dark Stranger who helps them to escape from the conditions of mortality. He leads them into the water gardens, which are Paradise Gardens, and into the company of the gypsies who are oblivious of the trammels of social convention, and directly in rapport with Nature. But the Dark Stranger is also a Fiddler, like the Devil, and the gypsies are Circe-like characters who seem in some ways sinister and minatory. The wordless choral music they sing in the Paradise Gardens is miraculously beautiful, inducing a pantheistic merging of ego-dominated passion into Nature, as does the wordless chorus in "A Song of the High Hills." But the young lovers' surrender is a surrender, not an act of triumph; they do not transcend, in making their own, the dark turmoil of passion which the Fiddler presumably is. Because the Eden of their childhood cannot be recovered they voluntarily surrender consciousness, slowly sinking their boat, allowing the waters to envelop them. The end of the opera is not a rebirth, or even a potential rebirth, from the waters, but a slow dissolution and relinquishment. This is why the orchestral summation, in "The Walk to the Paradise Garden," is miraculously poignant but consistently elegiac.

The village Romeo and Juliet surrender life because they cannot leave their childhood behind; Tristan re-experiences his childhood in order that he may live and die. The interdependence of love and death which both *Tristan* and *Götterdämmerung* sing of suggests how any composer looking to the future—not, like Delius, to the past—from the heights or depths of the Wagnerian crisis, had to seek a renewal of life within the psyche itself. We can observe the beginnings of this in one of Schoenberg's earliest works, the string sextet *Verklärte Nacht,* which was later transformed into a work for string orchestra. Although this piece is purely instrumental, it is a one-act, symphonically "subjective" opera on a theme closely related to *Tristan.* The poem by Richard Dehmel, which is translated into music, describes the walk of two lovers through the Dark Forest. She bears within her another man's child, possibly that of the husband she doesn't love; and the child is the burden of man's guilt. Walking through the darkness, and speaking with growing agitation of their awareness that their love must involve pain, they come upon a clearing in the forest which is "transfigured" by moonlight. Here they make love, and in the act of love the burden of guilt is assuaged, so that the child can be accepted as their own. This again is a regeneration myth, which has direct consequences in the music. To begin with, the texture is Tristanesque, though even riper and more sumptuous in its chromaticism, and the dialogue between high and low strings, representing the woman and the man, makes the operatic affiliations manifest. As the texture grows more harmonically agitated, however, so it grows more polyphonic; the Wagnerian sequences flow into a winging ecstasy, the "transfiguring" quality being in the whirling continuity of the lyricism and in the asymmetry of the melodic proliferations. In this sense *Verklärte Nacht* is a *positive* sequel to *Tristan,* as *A Village Romeo and Juliet* was not.

Despite the freedom of the polyphony, *Verklärte Nacht* contains no technical feature that is in itself revolutionary. Its conception of tonality is traditional: the D minor in which it opens is associated by Schoenberg, as by Beethoven, with the strife that is life's essence, while the D major in which it closes is a key of resolution; the moment of transfiguration is traditionally represented by an excursion into the high "sharpness" of F sharp. Nonetheless the linear independence of the music tends increasingly to override the Wagnerian sequences. And the more "air-borne" the polyphony becomes, the more the texture veers toward the ambiguous acceptance of chromaticism which, when once it is *unequivocally* accepted, will release us from the earth-pull of harmonic tension. This release comes in Schoenberg's "free" atonal period, and specifically in *Erwartung,* a work in which the literary theme is almost identical with that of *Verklärte Nacht.* The earlier piece was a "subjective" drama which takes place entirely in instrumental terms; in *Erwartung* the drama is, in a sense, theatrically objectified, but the implications of *Tristan* and *The Ring* are fulfilled, since there is now only one character, within whose mind the action takes place. Again, a woman is wandering, this time alone, through "the blind mazes of this tangled wood." She is possessed by a sexual passion of Tristanesque violence. Waiting to meet her lover in the wood, she knows at the same time that he will not come, that he has deserted her for a ghostly, white-armed other love who is probably, psychoanalytically speaking, his mother.

The climax comes when she stumbles upon his murdered body. It is not clear who murdered him; she refers, confusedly, to the other woman and to an indeterminate "they." But it is unclear because, of course, the action has no existence outside her own mind. She enters the dark wood of the unconscious, and the first stages of her wandering are a mingling of her memories and inchoate desires. Her discovery of the body is her recognition of loss, and complementarily of guilt and renunciation. From here on the unconscious takes over completely; text and music become hallucinatory, and "free" atonality is the musical synonym for this subconscious expressionism. Yet the pattern established by *Tristan* and *Verklärte Nacht* is continued, for submission to the unconscious brings release from terror; the piece ends with a "transfigured" vision of her lover, wherein passion is absolved, hatred forgotten. The absolution is also subjective. The point lies in her mind's and senses' aspiration; we don't know whether her love ever was or could be fulfilled in the conditions of temporality.

So the subjective fulfillment happens only in the music: which is why the text that Marie Pappenheim devised from Schoenberg's own suggestions is content to allow the music to re-create the fluctuations of the unconscious life; and is also why *Erwartung,* even more than *Tristan,* is a symphonic opera in which the drama takes place in the orchestra. The vocal line carries Wagnerian speech-song to a further point of melodic disintegration, as it follows the vagaries of the half-thinking, half-feeling mind; yet we have only to consider the first words the woman sings to see how the speech-rhythm, floating on the unconscious, has begun to counteract the earth-bound tug of meter and of harmonic symmetry. This fluctuating "additive" rhythm can be intimately related to the intense expressiveness of the orchestral texture which, in creating the atmosphere of the Dark Forest, creates too the realities of the imaginative life about which the woman is murmuring or crying in self-communion. For this reason the parlando line of the voice is not separate from the orchestral fabric. We find that, although the score contains a minimum of organization or repetition (since it is intended to express the gradual disintegration of mind and senses), the most dramatically crucial phrases which the woman sings are also those which attain greatest significance in the orchestral texture, and which recur not in exact recapitulation, but in evolutionary permutation. The phrase wherein, early in the opera, the woman says that if she cries out perhaps her lover will hear her, is echoed in the self-involved, undulating phrase wherein she admits he hasn't come. Alternating seconds and thirds are the basis of the extraordinary orchestral passage in which she panics, thinking she is pursued by black things of the woods, while the "cry" phrase reappears in anguished and modified inversion when she finds, or thinks she finds, her lover dead. This leads to the wonderful passage where she re-imagines her meetings with her lover in the walled garden (which, being a garden, and walled, is safe, compared with the forest's wildness). Here it is the luminosity of the orchestral texture that creates something like affirmation out of apparent dislocation, and this affirmative quality is never again lost, not even when she seems to be giving way to jealousy and nightmare. The climax of absolution comes when she asks "hast du sie sehr geliebt?" but can then add that he is not to blame. Perhaps one could almost say that during the course of the opera's "stream of consciousness" she learns that the tree trunk she had stumbled over (which let loose her nightmare) and the trunk of the murdered lover which she later discovers are the same. They are her own guilt, and she knows, like Tristan, that it was "I myself who brewed the potion." Then, with self-knowledge, the guilt can be lifted and, as morning glimmers through the blackness, she can have a vision in which she imagines she sees her lover, alive. The opera ends with her ineffably moving cry of longing, "Oh, bist du da? Ich suchte"; and the sensory life of the orchestral texture dissolves away in contrary motion chromatics.

It is difficult to know what to call this if it is not, as well as a moment of vision, an act of faith; and Schoenberg's music has demonstrated how the glimmer of faith is to be attained only by the relinquishment of consciousness, of corporeal rhythm, of thematic definition and of harmonic volition. The inner drama fades out in the flood of the unconscious, and in the final pages the orchestra transforms the Dark Forest into a water image. This dissolution into the gurgling waters harks back to the end of *The Ring* and of *A Village Romeo and Juliet* and looks forward to the waters that engulf Berg's Wozzeck, while his little child plays ball, as innocent of death as he is of whatever life has in store for him. It would be an exaggeration to say that this tremulously disembodied orchestral texture is a "positive" end, as compared with Delius's death-tending lament. It would, however, be true to say that the fluctuating, linear texture and radiant sonority of the Schoenberg and Berg passages contain at least the potentiality of a new birth. This mystical interpretation of the release from consciousness acquires explicit form at the end of *Die Jacobsleiter,* the gigantic oratorio that was to be the consummation of Schoenberg's "free" phase, though it remained (significantly) unfinished. The ladder of the title is the link between dying mortality and some kind of reincarnation, and the final passages of the score describe a woman on her deathbed who, having experienced the transition from life to death, floats upward, disembodied. The speaking voice becomes a wordless singing voice, winging over a dissolving orchestral texture that was to be distributed throughout the hall on loudspeakers, in a manner that we would now call stereophonic. Like the visionary moment in *Erwartung,* this transfiguration scene is not elegiac in feeling; and was, of course, a beginning as well as an end in compositional techniques, for the air-borne cantilena strikingly anticipates the melismatic vocal writing of Boulez.

This is clear if one considers *Pierrot Lunaire,* now generally accepted as one of the key works in twentieth-century music, as a successor to *Erwartung* and to Schoenberg's free atonal period in general. We are now a stage further away from Wagnerian heroism; the Hero has become a clown, the Pierrot-figure as symbol of Modern Man, and the rich sensory life of symphonic texture has given way to a chamber music idiom, usually thinly scored. The lyricism of the declamatory line has almost gone, too, for this Pierrot's song-speech, though freely notated as to pitch and duration, is now closer to speech than to song. Yet at the same time the Pierrot is a reincarnation of Tristan and of the Woman from *Erwartung;* though more broken and pathetic, he still yearns for love and the dream's fulfillment, and in nightmare imagines that he as lover has murdered the beloved. *Because* the voice can no longer sing, finding lyrical release, the instruments must seek the maximum of intensity from the minimum of physical force, so *Pierrot Lunaire* is a sequel to the Woman's cry of "Ich suchte," and if, in one sense, it is a piece about disillusion, it is also a search for Belief.

Since *Pierrot Lunaire* is in this sense a further twitch to the death-throes of humanism, we aren't surprised to discover that, within its humanistic "expressionism," it contains elements that might be described as ritualistic or even magical. The poems are grouped in three sets of seven, both magic numbers; and for the rest of his life

Schoenberg was to be haunted by number symbolism. It's as though he had to seek some cosmological certainty (mythical as much as mathematical) to offset his obsession with the flux; and this "mythology," like *Erwartung's* moment of vision, is discovered *through* submission to the unconscious. Similarly, the contrapuntal ingenuities that begin to appear as a substitute for orthodox harmonic and tonal criteria led inevitably to the serial principle. Even in the amorphous stream of *Erwartung* there is a hint of this, in that Schoenberg associates an ostinato figure with the *path* the Woman must take through the forest's obscurity. The ostinato is the Way, and so is the Row, when Schoenberg has arrived at his fully fledged serial principle, for even more than the Wagnerian leitmotif it fulfills some of the functions of an Indian raga in that both the melodic and the harmonic aspects of the composition are derived from it. It is the source of the composition's life, the element within which the creator's talent *must* manifest itself: in which sense the Row becomes, as Valen said it was, the Word of God, the certainty beyond the flux.

We can trace the transition to serialism within the sequence of *Pierrot Lunaire*. The first group of seven poems is formally the freest, the most *Erwartung*-like. If the Woman in *Erwartung* is Isolde in nervous disintegration, Pierrot is the Artist—indeed, Schoenberg himself—weary and sick with insatiable love-longing. Columbine, the woman and mate, cannot satisfy his yearning; he cannot laugh it away in the Dandy's frivolity; the romanticized love-dream turns into drops of blood on the lips of a consumptive; he cannot find religious sanction in offering his verses to the Madonna. It is significant that this first cycle ends with its seventh number, a poem wherein Pierrot is ill unto death with his unappeasable longing; that the music of this latter-day Tristan should be scored for speaking-singing voice with solo flute; and that the melismatic character of the flute line should be even more oriental in feeling than is the Shepherd's pipe in *Tristan,* largely because it is, in its chromaticism, further removed from harmonic implications. It is this monodic song—in which the "decadent" irony of the text becomes a means of achieving detachment from Self—that leads into the second cycle, wherein Pierrot descends into the Night of the unconscious and, in his broken and pitiful fashion, faces up to the images of guilt, crime and punishment, as Tristan and the Woman had had to. The wings of giant moths obscure the light of the sun; Pierrot sees himself as grave-robber, as blasphemer, as the murderer of love; and in the last song of the cycle imagines himself crucified for his guilt, the crucifiers being the Crowd or the World, his guilt being his verses. This set of pieces begins with a passacaglia wherein the rigidity of the ostinato saves Pierrot from madness as he is submerged in Night; elaborate contrapuntal devices are used, with similar intention, in all the songs of the group, and the solo flute monody returns at the emotional climax to the entire work—the instrumental interlude that links Pierrot's moon-vision to his crucifixion in the fourteenth song.

In this work the implicit equation between the Artist as Scapegoat and Christ is not taken up, for the third group of songs seeks for release from the agony of consciousness in fantasy: nostalgic reminiscences of the old Italian Comedy, dadaistic nonsense, and dreams of a fairy-world where guilt wouldn't matter. Naturally enough, the pieces are much freer; there are no embryonic serial pieces, except for "Moonspot," which, in its canonic complexities, seems almost parodistic—intentionally, for in it the spot (of guilt) which Pierrot tries to rub off his black jacket turns out to be moonshine. We can see here why *Pierrot* is so crucial a work in the history of twentieth-century music: the two complementary yet contradictory responses to the "crisis of humanism" are both implicit in it. Man could throw off consciousness as completely as is humanly possible, retreating to the Absurd, accepting the absurdity of life as itself a positive; or he could attempt to achieve a new integration of the splintered personality which could only be, at this stage in the checkered history of Europe, in some sense "religious." In the latter part of his career Schoenberg, like Freud, chose the second of these alternatives, and became a religious prophet. Both men were Jews, born about the same time, in the same city; both, in their life-work, started from the primary human urge of sexuality; both faced up to a hiatus in the flow of creative vitality that man's dedication to self had led him into. Freud sought to reintegrate the dislocated fragments of the personality; Schoenberg sought a linear and polyphonic (and later serial) integration of the chromatically splintered mind and senses.

The Jews, Owen Barfield has suggested (in *Saving the Appearances*), were a necessary link between the Ancient World and the flowering of Christianity—just as Jewish liturgical chant was an essential transition between oriental and Greek monody and the plainchants of western Europe. As against the oriental conception of Time as cyclic, the Semitic way was a progress forward through history, and it was a way "shared, indeed, by the individual but trodden by the nation as a whole." Only after the Greeks had "polarized creation into consciousness on the one side and phenomena, or appearances, on the other, was memory made possible, and it is through memory that man acquires his self-consciousness. The position of the Jews in history is comparable with the position occupied by memory in the composition of the individual man." Paradoxically Schoenberg, ultimate composer of the European consciousness of self, is also a composer of history, retracing the racial memory. In his earlier years he—identified with the Woman of *Erwartung* and with the lunar Pierrot—seeks to heal the breach between flesh and spirit created by post-Renaissance man's obsession with materiality; in his later work he attempts more radically to obliterate the mind's divisions, absorbing the Wagnerian yearning of his early music into a "mystical" resolution comparable with that of late Beethoven. His string trio and third and fourth quartets are the same kind of music as Beethoven's last quartets, with the important difference that Schoenberg's music fails to enter Beethoven's paradise; and like Beethoven, Schoenberg knew that if nameless terrors exist below the level of our consciousness, "God's kingdom is in ourselves" also. It is significant that, in the unfinished opera-oratorio *Moses and Aaron,* he saw this personal vision specifically within the context of the history of his race. This consummatory work stands in the same relationship to Schoenberg's serial period as the (also unfinished) *Die Jacobsleiter* stands to his free chromatic phase. The crisis within the inner life is now seen as an historical crisis also; in both, musical technique and philosophical statement are identical.

Like Freud, Schoenberg associates himself with Moses, as the revealer of the Spirit; yet he is also Aaron, the (necessary) mediator between God and the World, the instrument through which spirit might be made flesh. Though the human situation with which the opera deals is basic to the human predicament at any time and place, it has a painful pertinence to us today since, living at a time dedicated to materiality, we are acutely aware that any attempt at incarnation seems in some degree to sully spiritual revelation. Schoenberg demonstrates this, in his opera, in a characteristically uncompromising form, for all the "materials" of musical tradition become for him a partial betrayal. Thus he associates his most richly developed harmonic textures—his heritage from post-Renaissance Europe—with the World, and makes Aaron an operatic tenor, whose arioso often employs the row in harmonic contexts, with a prevalence of "sensuous" major and minor sixths. Similarly, the most powerfully "human" music in the score—the only music dominated by corporeal rhythms—is the "Dance Around the Golden Calf," which concerns man's ultimate degradation through his submission of the Idea to the Image. The horrid, lurching motor rhythms—the raucous, squealing orchestration, the realistically heterophonic polyphony—are images of chaos: "in the destructive element immerse." As a result, Schoenberg's erotic rite is not a positive impulse; if vigorously earthy, it is also sadistic, and the broken fragments of line and motive and rhythm are, at the height of the frenzy, disintegrative.

Yet in a sense this negative impulse is potentially also positive. Although Moses, in the biblical story, breaks the tables of the Law in anger at the people's idolatry, that idolatry is not wholly evil. The Golden Calf was also a Mithraic fertility symbol; in scattering his ashes upon the waters and then forcing the people to drink, Moses appealed directly to the dark forces which the Law would seem to deny. While this is never explicit in Schoenberg's music, one might say that in breaking up the animal rhythm of the body, the music yearns, in ecstatic inarticulateness, for transcendence. This is most notable in the unfrenzied, beautiful music sung to the Calf by the Old Men and the Invalid Women. Similarly, Aaron—who might be God's messenger—sometimes sings music which reminds us not of the row's material and sensual permutations, but of its divine origins, as he does, for instance, when he first "floated rather than walked" towards the people. The row itself—the Idea as against the multiple Images created from it—is here quite explicitly God: the alpha and omega of both the physical and spiritual universe, the ultimate unity of musical space in which, as Schoenberg himself said, there is no up or down, no right or left, no backward or forward, and no longer any tension, only suspension. The vertical form of the row which opens the opera on *wordless* voices has become, doctrinally, the Law, magically dividing the twelve semitones into four trinities of perfect and imperfect fourths (the Tristan chords) and of minor thirds and augmented fifths, producing chords which have the minimum of harmonic implication for the tonally trained ear. Similarly, the first horizontal statement of the row is a mirror structure with retrograde inversion—the serpent eating its own tail. The row, being God's eternity and infinity, could release us, as Moses *speaks* the Idea of the spirit's delivery, from consciousness and guilt. Yet the more Aaron the mediator *sings,* and the more he engages in musical and dramatic action, the more the melodic and harmonic properties of music become identified with the falling away from God, which culminates in the nervous and corporeal frenzy of the "Dance Around the Golden Calf." Aaron is perpetual change, and change, being of its nature mortal and ungodly, must involve corruption. This theme was implicit in Schoenberg's work as early as *Erwartung,* wherein the same neutral god-chords occur at the moment when the Woman has her transitory vision of peace and the Lover and Beloved become one in the safety of the Walled Garden, before the ultimate disintegration of mind and senses. Perhaps the end of *Erwartung* was the point at which Schoenberg relinquished the (Wagnerian) belief or hope—still latent in *Verklärte Nacht*—that the body's consummation might be also the spirit's grace.

Certainly it would seem that music, which for Schoenberg was essentially a search after Spirit, became in effect the Spirit's denial, completing Dryden's prophecy in "untuning the sky." Moses can only speak the Idea; Aaron in singing of it betrays it, while the people's vacillation, their lost state, is manifest musically in the fact that they exist in a no man's land between speech and song. The union of spirituality and corporeality—and therefore the spirit's fulfillment—cannot be achieved: so although Schoenberg's *text* for *Moses and Aaron* ends with the prophecy "In the wasteland you shall be invincible and shall achieve the goal: union with God," the last phrase that he actually set was "O Word that I lack,"* after which Moses sinks to the ground in despair. The orchestra's tritonal tensions coalesce in a unisonal F sharp on violins that swells to fortissimo, but then fades into silence; we are left with this momentary vision of the eternal unity, which neither Moses nor we can compass. It is difficult to imagine how the opera could have been completed since when, in the text of Act III, Moses reasserts the Idea, Aaron, though freed from the chains in which his denial of the Law had cast him, is liberated only to die. That Schoenberg, dually identified with Moses and Aaron, "fails" to lead his people into the Promised Land does not imply an artistic failure. On the contrary, one might say that it is because he experiences the spirit's revelation and the desire for its incarnation, yet cannot finally realize it, that the myth inherent in his life's work, and in *Moses and Aaron* specifically, is so immediately and deeply relevant to us. He wrote his most philosophically religious work at the time when he had temporarily renounced Judaism, because he had to face up to the crisis of humanism irrespective of any orthodoxy, inherited creed or *a priori* assumption. Like his Pierrot Lunaire, he became our scapegoat, purging our guilt in the fury of the Golden Calf episode, which is why we find the music so nervously, as well as physically, disturbing. Yet although Schoenberg does not himself achieve the new revelation and is in that sense an end to

* Schoenberg uses the terms Idea and Image as more or less synonymous with the Christian concept of the Word and the Flesh. His "Wort" is almost the opposite of St. John's Word that was in the beginning, for it is the means through which the Idea might be made manifest.

centuries of European humanism, it is clear that in reaching the ultimate inversion of humanism that was presaged in *Tristan,* Schoenberg's music could imply, for future generations, a fresh start. Harmonically based, even melodically founded, European music has proved to be a frustration of Spirit; and if Schoenberg did not himself ultimately explore the denial of the harmonic concept that is inherent in his musical synonym for God, Webern was to attempt precisely that, within the premises of serialism. The Jewish race, springing from the orient, made possible Christian humanism, which explodes in *Tristan* and *Parsifal;* Schoenberg, as Wagner's successor, reinstates Jewish consciousness and the duality of spirit and flesh; then his successors seek the supreme identity with the Brahma, wherein duality is meaningless.

For although Webern was a pupil of Schoenberg it would be true to say that from his earliest composing years his approach was in part non-Schoenbergian. Thus Schoenberg, who ultimately (as we saw) "inverted" European musical history, nonetheless started from the Beethovian and Brahmsian notion of music as Becoming: which notion we do not find even in Webern's opus 1, the *Passacaglia* for orchestra. Despite its obvious derivation from late Wagner, this work recreates Wagner in terms of Bach. Being a passacaglia, it is essentially a monothematic piece, on a D minor theme, including almost all the chromatic semitones, so that it is an anticipatory series. The technique throughout is that of monistic variation, the second motive being a crab or backward inversion of the first. The result is that, even in this opus 1, form is for Webern—much more consistently than for Berg or Schoenberg—the antithesis of development. It is interesting that if the *Passacaglia* reminds us of any then contemporary music it is of Mahler. Polyglot Vienna, at the end of the nineteenth century, saw the twilight of Western civilization, from the disintegration of which must come a rebirth within the psyche. Schoenberg, we have seen, was obsessed with the Wagnerian "subjective" crisis, with disintegration and reintegration within the ego itself. Mahler, though a fanatically self-revelatory composer, saw the self within the framework of civilization, and for him the symphony was a cosmos; he was concerned, both tragically and ironically, with the totality of the ego's experience, within a social context. Thus his last completed work, *Das Lied von der Erde,* is an elegy both on the Lost Self and on the world the self is lost in, and it is not an accident that the last movement should be a *farewell* both to the World and to Western consciousness. This is not a consequence of the fact that Mahler chose to set Chinese poems; on the contrary, he selected Chinese poems because he was concerned with this experience. The harmonic pulse of the music slows almost to immobility; the reverberation of percussion is separated by immense silences; the orchestration becomes luminous, linear, soloistic, as melismatic arabesques flower around ostinato notes and pedal points. These arabesques, predating Messiaen by thirty years, remind us both of oriental cantillation and of bird song, while the final chord, a Debussyan added sixth, is also a verticalization of the pentatonic scale.

The weeping appoggiaturas of the final pages of Mahler's *Das Lied* imply that the surrender of harmonic consciousness is reluctant; we weep for the self unfulfilled and the world lost, and can find in Mahler—an Austrian Roman Catholic Jew—a musical synonym for our own alienation and uprootedness. Webern's *Passacaglia* is almost exactly contemporary with Mahler's work, and resembles it in its luminous scoring, its rhythmic fluidity (largely created by triplet figurations sometimes stated, sometimes only implied, against a duple pulse), and in its use of silence. It differs from Mahler's *Das Lied,* however, because its stringent contrapuntal organization banishes lamenting nostalgia. In so far as it has a valedictory flavor it is more Brahms-like than Mahlerian. On the whole, however, we may relate it to the forward-looking, soloistic chamber-music polyphony of Mahler's work rather than to Mahler's regressive characteristics. We can already see why it was to be Webern, rather than Schoenberg, who was to create the new world of the spirit from which avant-garde music was to spring.

This brings us to the significant fact that Webern's early music is related to Debussy's revolution no less directly than to Schoenberg's. The *Five Pieces,* opus 5, for string quartet have obvious affinities with the tiny pieces of Schoenberg's "free" period, and like them relinquish sequence, repetition, architectural balance and dramatic argument. Yet they resemble the most Debussyan aspect of Schoenberg's earlier music, as exemplified by the piano pieces of opus 19, in each of which a "moment of sensation" is distilled, often from a single chord or interval. The fourth of Webern's five pieces carries this technique to a still more rarefied exquisiteness. Melody is a broken sigh, haloed by pedal notes and ostinati in harmonics. Despite its fragmentation, the music acquires a tender passivity more comparable with Debussy than with Schoenberg's nervous intensity; already it induces a characteristically Webernian calm.

This "seismographic," Debussyan quality is still more evident in the *Six Pieces* for orchestra, opus 6, which are the "Farewell" of Mahler's *Das Lied von der Erde* re-created not in epic terms but in terms of an exquisitely nervous inner life. It is interesting that even the comparatively extended, superficially agitated pieces, such as No. 2, use very short if pliant melodic phrases, repeated in obsessive rhythmic patterns, while the orchestral texture splinters into "points" of orchestral color, with single tones being repeated in complex numerical meters, like a tala. It's as though the melodic phrases are a last twitter of Western consciousness, which is dissolving into an oriental contemplation; and the use of the word "twitter" reminds us of Paul Klee's twittering machine and of the profound affinity there is between the minutely calligraphic art of painter and composer. Both Webern and Klee had deep roots in the past; yet if Webern would hardly have said, with Klee, that he wanted to be "as though new born, knowing nothing about Europe, nothing, knowing no pictures (or music or poems), entirely without impulses, almost in an original state," we can see that it is precisely some such liberation from the past that the young have found in him. The marvelous fourth piece from opus 6—composed as long ago as 1909—is in some ways closer to certain aspects of avant-garde music even than Webern's later work. It is in effect scored for two orchestras. One, immensely slow and almost pulseless, is an oriental orchestra of tolling gongs, bells and drums; the other, alternating sustained, gong-like ostinato chords on woodwind and thudding, funereal bumps on muted trombones and tuba with jittery, broken melodic phrases, rises to a kind of stifled scream: at which point Western consciousness expires, leaving the oriental percussion band alone.

The short, slow pieces (Nos. 3, 5 and 6) all use tiny, infinitely expressive melodic phrases which whimper into silence over ostinato chords on muted brass, or static ostinato figures on harp, celesta or string harmonics. Here it is not merely the individual chord, as in Debussy, which has become an end in itself; the isolated sound or tone-color has become an event, without antecedence or consequence. This tendency is still more marked in the *Five Pieces* of opus 10 (1913). Even briefer than the pieces of opus 6, these "moments of sensation" are now scored for very small forces, light and airy in sonority. The extraordinary third piece, with its quivery ostinato on mandoline and guitar, has no harmonic movement at all; the sound is startlingly suggestive of Japanese koto music.

The spontaneous affinity between Webern and the oriental and medieval mind in part explains why, when he began to write serial music, he tended to employ the row in a spirit different from Schoenberg's. For Schoenberg, the row was a refuge from chaos; the pressure of harmonic and tonal tension was so extreme that it had to be released into linearity. Webern, though highly wrought in nerves and senses, could live in and on his nerves in relative passivity; the explosive figurations that intermittently erupt in his music do not ultimately affect its radiance, nor even its serenity. This may be precisely what the music is "about": the music effects the catharsis of hypernervosity, in the same way as does Klee's meticulous, child-like, yet complex, quasi-oriental calligraphy. Webern can do this because, although rooted in humanist tradition, he was by nature a mystic: which is what Schoenberg frustratedly sought to be. This may mean that Webern is, for us, the more limited composer, but it also helps us to understand the curiously timeless perfection that his works achieve, almost from his earliest years.

It is interesting that when Webern scores the Ricercare from Bach's *Musical Offering* he makes it sound more medieval than baroque, for the presentation of the theme in "Klangfarben" style emphasizes its structure as a collocation of cells or tiny units and tends to deny the sense of growth. Webern makes the Ricercare not so much a religious piece in a social context—an equation between the human and the divine like most of Bach's music—but rather a still more hermetic version of the "abstract" rite of Bach's *Art of Fugue*. It's a religious piece, in that it seeks a haven of quiet within the mind: not a public affirmation of faith, but a private meditation wherein the contrapuntal unity is the oneness of God. Webern's own serial, especially canonic, processes are thus related philosophically as well as musically to the medieval aspects of Bach's art. Medieval contrapuntal unity is relevant to Webern's art, whereas Bach's "humanistic" ordering of harmonic tensions is not. Even in his most ostensibly Bachian work—the *Passacaglia,* opus 1—the contrapuntal process whereby the second motive is a backward inversion of the first is medieval, and in his serial works he has an instinctive partiality for the circular structure that is reflected, mirror-wise, into eternity. The rows he favors are not only more remote from tonal implications than Schoenberg's, they are also more mathematically ordered. For Schoenberg, the row was derived from the themes, a crystallization of melodic utterances; for Webern the row is a preordained structure within which, and only within which, creation may exist. In this sense, "what we establish is the law," as Webern has put it, and what is established (the row) is for Webern synonymous with what used to be called inspiration. Similarly, quoting Goethe, Webern has said that everything arbitrary or illusory must fall away: "here is necessity, here is God." So if the row is an abstraction, "the highest reality," it is also a revelation; and "a primal blessing shall come to bestow greater blessings."

The eternity-serpent dominates the form of many of Webern's later works; the *Piano Variations,* opus 27, gives us the row-theme accompanied by itself backward and inverted and, in the process, divests piano sonority of most of its traditional sensual appurtenances. The persistent major sevenths and minor ninths no longer have any effect of harmonic tension, but become a tinkling of bells surrounding melodic phrases that still have great expressivity, but are brief, broken, disembodied. If there is an oriental connotation in this, the music no longer has the directly sensuous appeal of the more Debussyan early works; corporeality has almost completely dissolved into spirit. The first movement of the *Symphony,* opus 21, for instance, has much in common with the techniques, and even the sonorities, of the late Gothic motet. The piece is in two symmetrical halves, both repeated, in double canon by inversion. While the material is, of course, chromatic not modal, the fragmentation of theme and motive, the "emptiness" of the texture, the dislocation of rhythms and the discontinuity of scoring all have their parallels in late Gothic technique. Then it was as though the preordained order of the cantus firmus and of the isochronous rhythms just held together the disintegrating fragments of a civilization, so that the music's seemingly suprapersonal order was at once austere and desperate. Here in Webern's *Symphony,* at the end maybe of the humanist phase of European civilization, Viennese (in particular Mahlerian) sensuality and pathos are reaching back to an order similarly preordained, and the more needed because European consciousness has traveled so far. And Webern succeeds—for himself, at least, and for us as participants in his private rite: for the final effect of this broken texture—in which "expressive" melody is fragmented into little sighs of two notes, or even into isolated single notes whose continuation is merely implied in silence—can validly be described as "ruhig." We can understand this more clearly if we consider the *Symphony* in relation to the sequence of vocal cantatas that were Webern's *opera ultima,* all of which have mystical texts, usually by Hildegard Jone.

Das Augenlicht, opus 26, being scored for four-part chorus with a chamber orchestra, reminds us that Webern was in fact a scholar in the field of late Gothic music, especially the motets of Matteo da Perusia. But his scholarly interest is a result, not a cause, of his creative instinct, for he too sought a quasi-mathematical, suprapersonal order from a texture (and experience) that was chaotically disintegrated. What was implicit in the *Symphony* is here explicit: the initial vocal entries in canon by inversion, the isolated sonorities of the individual notes in the instrumental parts, the silences within the triplet figurations that are often only latent, even the superhuman treatment of the human voice—all these have direct counterparts in the doctrinal or magical order and the hoqueting (or hiccuping) styles of late Gothic music. Moreover, the words of the text specifically concern "the light of the eye": how "one man's vision" may become miraculous, when light is born from the soul's retreat to the "sea's bed." The moment of vision becomes a moment of broken homophony; then the harmonic flesh finally disintegrates in the exquisite coda when the eyes open "und es macht ihn gut."

The mingling of Christian mysticism with pantheism which we find here is characteristic of all Webern's work, and may be responsible for the *affirmative* effect of many of his most abstract and—it would seem—nervously jittery compositions. The *Concerto* for nine instruments, opus 24, is a case in point. The piece has been much analyzed because its "machinery" is comparatively easy to describe. Thus it is based on the most symmetrical and mathematically ordered of all Webern's rows. What has not been pointed out, however, is that Webern's use of the row-material is part of an experiential process and that this—not the mere fact that serial-contrapuntal ingenuities exist—makes the piece good music. The segments of the row are initially hurled at us in a hierarchy of speeds. The rhythmic dislocations grow gradually more pronounced until the movement ends with a stretching out of the segments both in pitch and in rhythm (crotchet triplets against quaver triplets which often override the bar lines), followed by a brief coda stating all the segments in separation, and ending with a triplet hiccup across the beat. The total effect of this movement is thus highly nervous, like a cat on hot bricks.

By contrast, the second movement is almost completely immobile. The 2/4 movement is regular throughout, though it is complicated by the fact that some instruments move from strong to weak beat, whereas others move from weak to strong. This two-way pendulum creates a subtle sense of suspension and equilibrium. This is complemented by the fact that the harmonic texture keeps consistently to the alternation of thirds and major sevenths (chromatic semitones inverted) which is implicit in the row. Even more than in the *Piano Variations,* therefore, the dissonant harmony is deprived of its traditional tension; the dissolution of the melodic line, over the piano's pendulum, thus achieves, in this case, an oriental rather than medieval calm. Moreover, this immobility influences the nervosity typical of the first movement, for while the last movement is very quick and explosive, its canonic order is Gothic, and immediately apprehensible to the ear as well as the eye. Though the concept of development in the classical sense is irrelevant to Webern's work, it is true to say that there is an experiential process, if not progress, in this piece: because of our entry into the slow movement's timeless heaven we can reassert a kind of corporeal rhythm, and when that in its turn becomes broken and disrupted, we can find in the process a kind of gaiety, even hilarity, for the hoquets at the end of the movement remind us of a jazz break: nor is the comparison facetious, since the jazz break seeks ecstasy from the beat's destruction. If this movement is comedy, it is high comedy which tunes with Webern's mysticism and reminds us that he still has the essential humanity without which sublimation becomes meaningless.

Discovering in abstraction "the highest reality," Webern in a limited sense succeeded where Schoenberg, in *Moses and Aaron,* had failed. As a human testament, Schoenberg's failure may be more significant than Webern's success, but it was the apparently consummatory nature of Webern's achievement that led to his becoming a seminal figure, whose music in part precipitated the new world of the avant garde. Webern's abstraction was not, however, the only possible extension from Schoenberg. Other composers were to follow through the implications of that haunted and haunting flute monody from *Pierrot Lunaire,* and of the surrealistic tendencies of the songs in the third cycle. This surrealism could be and was allied to certain features of the music of Claude Debussy, that other great seminal figure whose revolution is in some ways even more radical than that of Schoenberg. In the technique of Schoenberg we have observed the disintegration of the burden of harmonic passion inherent in the Wagnerian sequence, its attempted sublimation, and its ultimate frustration, until it finds a kind of release in the abstraction of Webern, Schoenberg's disciple. Now in Debussy's music Wagnerian sensual passion is still (harmonically) evident; but al-

III

The Dark Forest: Debussy's *Pelléas et Mélisande* as a Parable of Relinquishment

In Wagner's *Tristan und Isolde* the identity between love and death is the beginning of the end of humanism. For Wagner, it is a triumphant end, for though Tristan has to die, he dies in the belief that his consuming passion is the universe. That was a heroic achievement. More naturally, the twilight of humanism led to a pessimistic view of human destiny; this is evident both in Maeterlinck's play of *Pelléas et Mélisande* and in Debussy's almost verbatim setting of it. For though the theme is the same as that of *Tristan,* the treatment of it could hardly be more different. Wagner wrote the libretto of *Tristan* himself, directing it toward the music which, in its continuous flow, is his own inner life. The music is the shaping reality, which achieves its triumph even as it seems to be driven by forces outside the Self—by Time and by Fate (what happens to us). Debussy, on the other hand, sets the play as a play, allowing the music the minimum of energy as a shaping force. Technically, his approach returns to Monteverdi's conception of opera as a play in music, making allowance for the fact that Monteverdi expected heroic actors to declaim, whereas Maeterlinck's language and Debussy's setting of it—coming at the end of the cycle of European humanism—dethrone the Hero and are naturalistic in expression. This is a logical extension of Wagnerian technique, for Wagner's song-speech would have been naturalistic if he and his characters had not been supermen.

If we compare Debussy and Schoenberg as successors to Wagner, we see that, for Schoenberg, retreat to the unconscious had to lead to a mystical vision, a renewal of the religious instinct, however thwarted. For Debussy, however, the state of will-lessness becomes a good in itself. This distinction is evident in the orchestral texture of *Erwartung* and of *Pelléas et Mélisande*. Both Schoenberg and Debussy start from Wagner's orchestral sensuality, both achieve from it an exquisite refinement that does not cease to be sensual. Yet the "expressionist" concentration of Schoenberg's harmony is created from a texture that is increasingly linear and, in that sense, harmonically disintegrative. The "air" which he thus lets into the Wagnerian cocoon gives to the texture the typical radiance on which we commented, and this sonority is inseparable from the work's approach toward a metaphysical vision. If Schoenberg frees the Wagnerian leitmotives still further into linearity, Debussy does the opposite, for although the texture is softer and more delicate than Wagner's, it is still more pervasively enveloping. It feels like a release because the Wagnerian desire egoistically to shape the themes and mold the sonority has gone; we live and move—insofar as we move at all—within the mists of the unknown that surrounds us. In a sense the sonority is the All, to which, however intense our passions, we can do no more than react seismographically.

This is evident in every aspect of the technique. Thus, whereas Wagner's "endless melody," though repeatedly frustrated, is always sequentially pressing onward, seeking the ultimate resolution of the Tristan chords' tension in the Shepherd's monodic piping and the melodic consummation of the "Liebestod," Debussy's leitmotives tend to be isolated from one another, even to be restricted to separate scenes, and although they change, they do not grow. Complementarily, his sensuously undulating harmonies, his Wagnerian chromatics, differ from Wagner's in that they do not even seek to progress. They oscillate around fixed nodal points; thus, the harmonic sensuality is paradoxically unrelated to *corporeal* energy, and the *spiritual,* numerical rhythm of the vocal line (which is closer to plainsong than to operatic recitative) floats, directionless, on the sensual harmonies. The static nature of the harmony, combined with the melismatic, usually pentatonic, arabesques into which the melodic lines flower, often gives Debussy's music an oriental flavor, which derives not from the superficial fact that he heard Javanese music at the Paris Exhibition, but from his intuitive need to counteract "the pain of consciousness" with an oriental passivity. In Wagner, the inner life tries to take control, to become the universe, and in Schoenberg the spirit seeks, if it does not find, ecstasy through the unconscious. In Debussy, retreat to the inner life becomes a surrender to destiny. We are lost, will-less, in the dark wood, and to accept this as the essential human condition is the only wisdom we can hope for. It doesn't matter that God as creator or as preserver is absent. Instead of God, there are feelings, sensations, and whatever causes sensations. Accepting the flux, human consciousness is reduced to existence without duration. There is only the present moment, no causation and no consequence; the revolution in Debussy's world lies in the fact that this condition no longer induces terror.

The profound difference between this surrender and that in Delius's *A Village Romeo and Juliet* is that in Delius the sense of Wagnerian harmonic progression still implies the will to desire, however frustrated it may be, and still involves memory of happiness past. Debussy, more radically, seeks to release consciousness from both memory and desire; this is why his opera is so disturbing and has had so deep an effect on the history of our time. We can see this in Maeterlinck's treatment of the myth itself. The story of *Pelléas* is very close to that of *Tristan,* with one crucial distinction. The climax of *Tristan,* we saw, was the hero's immense soliloquy, his traumatic Delirium, wherein he admitted that the responsibility for drinking the potion was his alone; thus *he* is Fate, and the recognition is both his death and his triumph. *Pelléas* reverses this. Golaud—the only character who attempts to take action about anything—is the villain, though a sympathetic villain because he is a part of us, as King Mark is a part of Tristan. For the young lovers the only happiness consists in submission, and since they do not even know what they are submitting to, submission becomes at the end identified with inanition.

Since Debussy seeks freedom from memory and desire, *Pelléas et Mélisande* takes place in a timeless antiquity which is also an eternal present, and in a *selva oscura* which is also the subconscious and the world of dream. The first sounds we hear are those of a slow, march-like theme, built on a rising fifth, which in the Middle Ages was God, but now is Destiny, taking precedence over all. Imposed on it is Golaud's theme, which would imply action in its syncopated rhythm, yet revolves on itself, unable to break away from its obsessive anchor D, and then peters out over neutral whole-tone chords which are an ellipsis of two Tristanesque tritones, no longer attempting resolution. Mélisande's theme first appears over a pedal note, in whole-tone harp arpeggios; incapable of growth, her tune is pentatonically innocent and drifts, rudderless, on the whole-tone flow. Golaud finds her, weeping, by a well: the source of spiritual life from which everyone is cut off. He tells her that he was out hunting, but his prey—a wounded boar—escaped. Since we learn later that he was in fact on his way to make an important marriage, for reasons of state, we may suspect that this boar was phallic, and that even Golaud, the man of action, acts to no end. Lost in the Dark Forest through Experience which he cannot understand, he lights on Mélisande, who is no less lost through her Innocence. She runs away from him in pentatonic scurrying and says she will throw herself into the well if he attempts to touch her. She would return to "spirit" because she fears the contagion of the world, by which, she tells us in a quivering of pentatonic thirds, she has been irremediably "hurt." The hurt, apparently, explains why she has lost the Golden Crown that an anonymous "he" had given her, as she is later to lose Golaud's ring, and any hope of sensual fulfillment. Most significantly, when Golaud, as potential man of action, offers to recover the crown for her from the water, she won't hear of it, but breaks into hysterical protest. She doesn't want to be "whole," and this in part explains the extraordinarily potent effect of the "innocence" of Debussy's recitative.

It is interesting that in this initial scene the vocal lines don't change in character as the exchanges between Golaud and Mélisande become more passionate. The harmony grows more distraught, the orchestral texture suggests a suppressed agitation by cross-rhythms, but floating in whole-tone sequences the music acquires no harmonic momentum, and the vocal lines, murmuring in speech-inflected, pentatonic incantation, are powerless to direct the incipient flood of passion. Despite the incessant chromatic oscillations, the only real modulation in this scene is the shift to a whole-tone pentatonic F sharp when Golaud at last tells Mélisande his name, and she, faced with the fact of human identity, becomes immediately conscious of mortality, and remarks that his hair is graying. Over an obsessive syncopated rhythm he tells her that they can't stay in the wood forever, his "hunting call" theme linking him with both destiny and the possibility of action. Despite his clarified, A-flat-majorish lyrical expansion, she says she will do *nothing*. Passive again, however, she finally agrees to go with him if he will promise not to touch her.

The next scene takes place six months later. Mélisande, her innocence presumably submitting passively to his experience, has married Golaud, and it is significant that we are aware of this temporary triumph of Golaud's activity over Mélisande's passivity in the orchestral interlude *between* the scenes. We hear of the situation from a letter which Golaud has written to his half brother Pelléas, and which Geneviève, his mother, is reading to King Arkel, his grandfather. She reads, in pentatonic incantation, like someone telling an old tale, with an occasional intrusion of a diminished fourth (on the word "sanglote," for instance) reminding us of the vibrant reality of passion, even if we are directionless. Golaud confesses, in the letter, that he found Mélisande in the Dark Forest when they were both lost, and that he knows no more about her now than he did when they married. He fears that Arkel will not approve of the marriage, and asks Pelléas to light a lantern on the tower that overlooks the sea if all is well. If he sees no light, he will sail away and never return home; even the man of action, apparently, is craven.

When Geneviève has finished the letter, the orchestra sighs a Tristanesque phrase built on a rising fifth and drooping appoggiatura which takes the place of what Arkel cannot bring himself to utter. The phrase appears in various forms, always nondeveloping, while Arkel says that he doesn't like the marriage and had hoped that Golaud would have effected his marriage of social convenience, especially since his father and acting king is sick, and probably dying. Nonetheless, Arkel never battles against fate; what must be, will be, and there may be a pattern in destiny which we cannot perceive. Arkel's theme, rising up a fourth and then descending, is faintly liturgical, without Golaud's whole-tone vacillations, for he is the closest Debussy's world can come to quasi-divine sanctions. Not surprisingly, the theme is related to the Fate motive, both in its contours and in the regularity with which it is repeated. Though fateful, it is not sinister, but tenderly compassionate.

Arkel, if wise, is significantly almost blind: in so far as we see truly, we cannot see much. Pelléas, who now enters, is the grandson of Arkel and the son of Geneviève by the Dying King, whereas Golaud is Geneviève's son by a previous husband, long dead. Pelléas's youthfulness is thus contrasted with the "gray-haired" experience of his half brother, and he sings music which has a simple animation, if not energy; his life-enhancing qualities are associated with a characteristically eager, syncopated rhythm, and with the "sharp" key of E. But his music, too, is obsessed with ostinato figures and with oscillations between two tonally neutral chords, so that it never "gets anywhere" harmonically. The first thing he tells us is that he has been summoned to visit a dying friend—which may be a premonition of his own death. Arkel persuades him not to leave, since his king and father is dying also, and the scene ends when they hang the lantern on the tower, to light home Golaud and Mélisande. The simplest pentatonic version of the Mélisande theme provides a reticent, if subtle, extension to fluttering harp arpeggios and bell noises. In the interlude the music takes over, becoming—as it does in *Tristan* and in *Verklärte Nacht*—the life of the psyche. Here the ostinati and harmonic "nodes" turn into a more Tristan-like chromaticism, and although the music never promises anything like Tristan's final affirmation that comes *from* frustration, the energy and yearning are the more desperate for being caged in two-bar periods. The interlude brings Golaud and Mélisande over the unknown sea; and although she and Pelléas haven't yet met, their love and their fate are, in the interlude, already preordained.

In the next scene Mélisande, having arrived at the castle, is talking with Geneviève about the gloom of the forest which surrounds the castle. They are all in darkness, blind. She wanders to the seashore through an opening in the forest in order that she may seek some light. But the sea itself is shrouded: a tempest is raging far out, and undulating ninth chords combine with a distant, ghostly sailors' chorus to suggest the flux of the natural, and perhaps supernatural, world. Pelléas comes to look for her, and together they think they see, through the mist, lights that might be a guide. But these lights are all dubiety, as was, perhaps, the lantern that had summoned her and Golaud home. Hints of the high, sharp love-keys of E and F sharp dissolve in vaporous tremolando ninths, and in echoes of Golaud's hunting theme. The orchestra's storm stops when Pelléas tries to take Mélisande's hand to lead her back to the castle. But she cannot touch him, she says, for her arms are full of flowers. The miraculous lyrical effloresence of the phrase, as opposed to the speech-norm of the recitative, gives incarnation to the words, and is the beginning of their love. But it fades to silence in a mingling of the sea-mist music with the love song, with added sixths echoing around an F-sharp-major triad.

If Golaud is the Flesh and the Will and Mélisande Spirit, Pelléas is perhaps potentially their union, and therefore what each needs. The next scene certainly suggests that the fulfillment of sexual love could be the spirit's renewal, for it takes place in a park, by a fountain. To luminous E-major-based music, but with no harmonic movement, Pelléas speaks to Mélisande of the fountain's miraculous properties. It used to be called "Blindman's Well" because it cured blindness; but it does so no longer, and Arkel himself is nearly blind. The "religious" note is suggested by hymnic distonic concords, the failure of spirit by undulating chromatics. Softly, tenderly, the young people begin to indulge in love play and Mélisande tries, but fails, to touch the water with her life-fearing hands, though her long hair can just reach it. Pelléas tells her of how Golaud had found her by a fountain, just as he has; reminiscences of Golaud's music induce agitation in her and she drops Golaud's ring, with which she had been playing, into the water. She has lost the life fulfillment Golaud might have been, if she had ever found it. The water noises, as the ripples settle down, are all whole-tone uncertainty, and the Golaud theme takes over in the next orchestral interlude, which is the longest thus far, and the most Wagnerian in intensity, though it is still in part immobilized by pedal notes.

The dark realities of passion are now released in music that is not the less disturbing for being irresolute. Golaud is telling Mélisande how he had an accident while riding; at the stroke of twelve (when Mélisande dropped the ring), his horse stumbled, and the water splashing of the previous scene is the stumble. He felt as though the woods were closing in on his body. Mélisande sobs in her "hurt" pentatonic thirds, but denies that her misery has anything to do with Pelléas; it's just that the castle is so old and dark, and everyone is dying. She cannot accept the fact that action is inevitably subject to decay, just as, when she and Golaud first met, she had been frightened by his graying hair. Golaud, taking her hand to comfort her (though he says he could *crush* it), notices that her ring is missing. This takes us immediately into the world of action; his agitated questioning in cross-rhythm is at first almost entirely unaccompanied, but grows increasingly fervent, harmonically, though it is still without direction since the harmonic patterns are nondeveloping ostinati. Mélisande pretends that she lost her ring in a cave by the sea (with patent Freudian implications), and Golaud insists that she go at once to look for it, taking Pelléas with her if she's scared! To an acute harmonic tension, Golaud says that Pelléas will do anything she asks, won't he? and Mélisande goes out crying how unhappy she is, to the same falling thirds as had expressed the first efflorescence of love.

So Pelléas and Mélisande descend together to the sea's depths and to the womb. The interlude mingles Pelléas's yearning motive with the fountain's pentatonic innocence, but dissolves both in undulating chromatic sea noises as they enter the cave. When they are in darkness—in the obscurity of a modal C-sharp minor which is the *relative* of Pelléas's daylight E major—we know that they had no choice but to make their dark pilgrimage, pointless though it seems, since they both knew that the ring is not and never was in the cave. As they go further in, the music modulates vaguely, and Pelléas tells her not to be afraid, for they will stop when they can no longer see any light from the sea. Then, in the depths, Mélisande gives a yell as a sudden shaft of moonlight reveals three (once more highly Freudian) white-haired paupers, starving remnants of famine in the land. The whining, medieval parallel fifths in the orchestra, unharmonically related, are a striking musical image for the withering of life both within the psyche and in the external world. How closely the inner and outer life are connected is indicated by the tentative reappearance of Golaud's music of action; Mélisande's love becomes nightmare because it cannot be realized in action, while the external world starves because it cannot embrace love. One could almost say that this opera is directly "about" the sundering of body and spirit and the consequent death of both.

So the lovers' descent into the waters and the cavern of the womb only *seems* to lead to love's consummation. They know they have to make the descent, and the reason is not the footling one that Pelléas gives (the necessity for Mélisande to be able to describe the cave to Golaud). Yet they explore the cave like children, almost as a self-scarifying game. This is probably why Mélisande is so terrified by the beggars revealed by the transfiguring moon; she can't stand the light of illumination, yet can't accept the dark in lieu of the light of day. Pelléas says he'll take her back before the light from the sea has totally vanished, and that maybe "nous reviendrons un autre jour"—the child's habitual "tomorrow." With the sundering of flesh from spirit and the decay of volition, the love scene that opens the third act, though complementary to the love nocturne in the second act of *Tristan,* becomes a consummation in dream, not reality. The image of Mélisande isolated in her tower emphasizes this. She croons to herself a folk-like incantation about her yellow hair, based on the oscillating thirds of her "hurt" motive and accompanied by orchestral night noises. The lyricism is beautiful and heart-easing; yet its ballad-like simplicity makes her seem a little girl, or a fairy princess, rather than a woman. This chant is in a Dorian E minor, complementing Pelléas's E major, and its monodic innocence brings in the opera's only reference to Christian sanctions. Perhaps this further emphasizes the division between spirit and flesh, for when Pelléas comes in to tell her (as he does at intervals throughout the play) that he must leave tomorrow, Mélisande can't decide whether she's glad or sorry. She cries "No, no"; but though she leans toward him from her tower, she cannot touch him with her hands—just as, leaning over the well, she had been unable to bathe her hands in the water. Her hair, however, cascading down the tower, does just reach him as he climbs toward her, in the same way as her hair had dabbled in the well-water which her hands could not contact. Enveloped in the whirl of her hair, Pelléas finds a kind of rapture. That the rapture is qualified is suggested by the fact that Mélisande is startled by an object in the darkness which she thinks may be a Rose (of sexual fulfillment?), though Pelléas, not altogether surprisingly, doubts whether it is a rose at all. Thus Pelléas's music in this love scene grows increasingly extended and lyrical; it is almost possible to speak of a climax when the music modulates from Pelléas's E major to F sharp, the key of heightened consciousness, here enharmonically noted as G flat. Yet the flatness, in this most beautiful music, seems to make a difference, since the tender lyricism does not achieve a mating of spirit and flesh. The music representing Mélisande's cascading hair is significantly related to her "hurt" minor thirds, and at the climax of his passion she utters another yell and complains that he is causing her pain. The love theme sounds more tenuously as doves fly around them in the gloom. The modal C-sharp minor which is reality, as compared with the bliss of E-major heaven—is interrupted by footsteps and, to a hushed, expectant rhythm, Golaud enters. As his hunting theme sounds distantly he (self-protectively) calls the lovers silly children, and leads Pelléas away. The interlude mingles Golaud's theme with Pelléas's yearning, and is suspended, unresolved, around the transfiguring key of F sharp.

Now it is the turn of Pelléas and Golaud to descend to the depths, and we begin to understand how the opera is concerned with a life failure in all the marvelously "realized" central characters. Mélisande's innocence could not accept Golaud's experience and because of this failure she cannot be renewed by Pelléas's love: she cannot find the Rose for the Thorn. But if Mélisande's spirit has never found a body, Golaud's "corporeal" experience has lost touch with spirit; so he can find no answer to his crisis of jealousy—whether or not it be justified—except madness and despair. He descends with Pelléas into the vaults of the castle, where the water isn't even living like the sea, but is stagnant, with the stench of death. In a sense, he seems to be playing a kind of game, as did Pelléas and Mélisande in their descent to the sea cavern; and his grimmer game seems to be the consequence of the separation of his will from love, for he deliberately frightens Pelléas by flickering his lantern. This must be why his descent—like that of Mélisande—only *seems* to be a prelude to a moment of illumination and forgiveness.

As they return to the light, the cascading whole-tone arpeggios on harp become "air from the sea," and the breezes mingle with the smell of freshly watered roses and the sound of bells in a pentatonic F sharp. Children are bathing in the sea, and there, too, is Mélisande, with Geneviève. Musically this is, and is meant to be, a miraculous moment. Dramatically, however, it is tragic irony, for after Golaud has remarked that he knows all about Pelléas and Mélisande but recognizes that it's only child's play, he himself exploits the child-innocent motive to sinister purpose. Golaud cross-questions Yniold, his little son by his first marriage: is Mélisande often with Pelléas? What do they talk of, what do they do? Golaud's music is all speech inflection, with no song left; Yniold's answers are in the simplest pentatonicism, like a nursery incantation. Significantly, Golaud's questions are accompanied by the whole-tone "vaults" music, the revelation of the horror beneath the surface of the mind, until at the climax of this nagging the vault motive turns into a febrile version of Mélisande's "hurt" thirds, and he painfully crushes Yniold's arm, as he had longed to crush Mélisande's hand. Experience, by itself, seems as inadequate as Innocence, for Golaud breaks down and says he is a *blind man,* stumbling across the sea floor, searching for his *lost gold* (his ring, and Mélisande's hair).

The contrast between the innocence of Yniold's pentatonic nursery music (rather Moussorgskian in flavor) and Golaud's frenzy grows more acute as his questioning continues. The climax comes when he sets the boy to spy on the lovers through a little window. Yniold says they're doing nothing, just standing, looking; he must get down or he'll scream. Golaud's frenzy is expressed in short, self-revolving phrases in whole-tones; he again hurts Yniold as he tugs him down from the window and the act ends brusquely, with unisonal tutti on the "hurt" motive inverted—in a Phrygian E minor, as opposed to Pelléas's E-major paradise.

The "positive" elements in the fourth act are thus again in part tragic irony. Pelléas, returning to his static E major, makes an assignation to meet Mélisande, before he finally leaves, by Blindman's Well. It is not clear why he is leaving: whether in response to Golaud's warnings, or to succor his dying friend, or from an incapacity to face the consequences of passion or, most probably, from a mixture of all these motives. The water ripples of the fountain figure, which dominate this scene, have in any case acquired a certain suppressed agitation, because love seems of its nature to involve pain: Pelléas hurts Mélisande in loving her, Mélisande hurts Golaud, and Golaud hurts Yniold, perhaps as a scapegoat. The inescapability of pain and death is recognized in the crucial scene in the opera when Arkel, in the heightened sharpness of B major, speaks to Mélisande of the new life she has brought to the castle through her youth, beauty and innocence. Because of this, he says, the Dying King seems to be recovering: but he is not so much hinting at a rebirth as saying that only the apprehension of beauty can make it possible for us to bear the fact of death. So his passively fateful theme is exquisitely intertwined with the love theme, high up, in E major, and the fatefulness is stronger than the love. His song of affirmation, being still anchored by pedal points, has no real movement; and movement is life. So gradually the love theme changes into the theme of Golaud, who appears with blood on his brow. He speaks brusquely to Mélisande, as the E-major lyricism ceases. More peasants have been inconveniently dying of starvation around the castle, he testily remarks; then he turns to the death within himself, taunting her about her innocent eyes, growing increasingly hysterical in obsessive repeated notes and neurotic whole-tone scurryings. Now it is he who says that Mélisande must not touch *him,* for he cannot bear the contagion of flesh. He, too, cannot take her hands, but only her long, gold hair, which he seizes ferociously, haling her up and down, forcing her to her knees: the lid is off the libido, indeed. When Arkel comes back he regains control, but we are left with Mélisande's broken "Je ne suis pas heureuse," and with the sighing appoggiaturas that comment on Arkel's statement that, if he were God, he would have pity on human suffering. As a mere human, albeit a king, he can feel for human beings, but do nothing. He is more fortunate than Golaud, Pelléas and Mélisande only because he is very old, and to that degree habituated to suffering.

The next scene is introduced simply to demonstrate this inescapability of destiny. The man is father to the child, the child is father to the man; little Yniold, the next generation, is trying to move a great stone, behind which he has lost his *golden ball,* as Golaud had lost his golden ring (his arm isn't long enough to reach it, as Mélisande's hand couldn't touch the water, and Pelléas couldn't stretch up to her in her tower). A flock of sheep pass by, crying. The unseen shepherd, asked where they are going and why they're crying, says they're not going to the stable, that's certain. He and they disappear into the mist. This scene, outside the action, is musically the most continuous in the opera. Rhythmic continuity and simple lyricism, like nursery songs, can live in the preconscious world of childhood, but, depending on incantatory repetition, they cannot develop. The point seems to be that as we grow up we lose even this lyrical self-sufficiency. We disintegrate into fragments, like the flock of sheep, at once one and many, fading into the mist. The scene peters out in a drooping minim figure, an inversion of the original nursery motive.

It is at this point that Pelléas enters and admits that he has been playing "like a child," knowing no more than the sheep what he was doing nor where he was going. He must go away, like a *blind man* leaving a house that is burning down, not because he would not love if he could, but because he doesn't know what is reality and what illusion; significantly, he says he cannot remember what Mélisande looks like. When she arrives for their assignation, they attain a moment of utter stillness and speechlessness which is the closest they come to illumination. But the very slow, lyrical expansion of the music after the castle gates have shut them out merges the love theme, the water motive and Golaud's hunting theme with the bare fifths of fate. From the "heightened" stillness of F-sharp major the music moves into an almost Wagnerian climax, though with very brief, panting phrases. This is the lovers' only real physical contact, apart from Pelléas's playing with Mélisande's hair; and (Parsifal-like) his confession of love is also a renunciation—he must go *because* he loves her, which, as we have seen, is only part of the truth. For all his dubiety, they touch F-sharp major again, just before Golaud, chasing them, slays Pelléas, and Mélisande scuttles off into the dark ("je n'ai pas de courage"). The end is abrupt, in F minor, after the F-sharp-major climax and the whirling chromatics.

So Mélisande has failed to grow from her innocence to experience, to give her Spirit a bodily consummation; Golaud has failed to renew his experience in her innocence, so that his Flesh turns destructive and sadistic; and Pelléas, the half brother and the lover who might have grown to love and life, is slain by their failure, which is inseparable from his own. We don't know what happened outside the castle gates, before the frenzied Golaud's approach; but if the lovers' passion is finally consummated in their last moment of F-sharp-major illumination, when Pelléas speaks of hearing Mélisande's voice float over the sea, in spring, the consummation is in no sense a triumph. More probably, their love is not consummated, and the moment of revelation is a dream of what might have been. In any case, the murder of Pelléas does not lead to his mystical union with the beloved. She, wounded in the affray when Pelléas is killed, dies not of her wound but because the pulse of life, with the failure of love, gradually slows to inanition. The last act opens at her deathbed, with a tremulous, frail, chromatically altered version of the Mélisande theme which sounds through the act like a knell. Interestingly enough, this theme—with implicit false relations and whole tone ambiguities wherein the A flats sometimes "stand for" G sharp—is very similar to the ostinato theme that dominates the neutral "waste-land" finale of Vaughan Williams's *Sixth Symphony.* Both the chromatic alterations and the regular, pulseless repetition give it a raga-like oriental quality. Passion, having been consistently destructive, is spent. Golaud, penitent, admits that they were innocent, he guilty, as fragments of his theme wander disconsolately in the bass, and the whole-tone fountain motive quivers on top. Mélisande, accompanied by diatonic concords, asks for the window to be opened, so that she may watch the sun setting on the sea. Arkel asks if Golaud may speak to her; she says Yes, there is nothing to forgive. The knell undulates chromatically as everyone leaves except Golaud. The orchestra stops and he asks her a question: did she and Pelléas love one another? he has to know. She says Yes, to which he replies that she doesn't understand. He means did he love her bodily; she must tell him the truth, for she is going to die and cannot die on a lie. So despite his repentance, the horror returns, and the fateful, obsessive-rhythmed seventh chords turn into whole-tone hysteria again. It seems we can never undo the consequences of our mistakes. She whimpers "la vérité . . ." and relapses into unconsciousness. So he, and we, never know "la vérité" and this, it would seem, is the essence of the human condition. There is neither a physical nor a metaphysical consummation, only an intense capacity to feel, and an oriental passivity in the acceptance of the unknowable mysteries of birth and death, and of the fact of human suffering.

So to speak of failure, in this twilight of humanism, is perhaps hardly relevant. We are all like Mélisande, deluded by our innocence and, like Golaud, corrupted by our experience; and so, like Pelléas, we never fully realize our love, because we cannot recognize it, or distinguish truth from falsehood. And the end of the opera tells us that this is a perennial human destiny. Arkel prevents Golaud from attempting to waken the unconscious Mélisande and the servants enter in ritualistic procession, to pray as Mélisande dies, while the knell slows to immobility, continually returning to Pelléas's

E, but with an oppressed, flattened, Phrygian feeling. She tries to hold her newborn baby (presumably Golaud's), but is too weak to do so. Arkel utters an exquisite benediction on suffering humanity and, in the final words of the opera, says "C'est au tour de la pauvre petite." The babe is born, and life will go on, but the next generation will weep the same tears anew. We hear those tears as the music peters out in fragments of the fountain's whole tones and the Mélisande love theme. In the last few bars the cycle starts again, for the simplest, most innocently pentatonic version of Mélisande's theme has re-emerged from the chromaticized knell, while the sighing appoggiaturas of the fountain scene have become the *lacrimae rerum*. The static, moveless tonality is C-sharp major, the highest, sharpest point of illumination in the opera. Perhaps it is not fortuitous that this key is the major form of the minor key which had been "reality," relative of Pelléas's paradisal E major. The concept is profoundly oriental: only through shedding the not-self can the Reality beyond our earthly passions be apprehensible.

Yet if the revelation is at hand for the dead Mélisande, what we are left with is Arkel's quietly compassionate fortitude; if the bell tolling has a ritualistic flavor, it is a ceremonial elegy on humanism. *Pelléas et Mélisande,* the quintessence of Debussyan technique and of the Debussyan theme, is one of the supreme seminal works of the twentieth century because both its passion and its relinquishment are uncompromising. It offers no heroic apotheosis (like Wagner), no metaphysical hope (like Schoenberg), no refuge in nostalgia (like Delius); but it does leave us purged, and for that reason ready to go on living. It can do this because of the intensity of its awareness of human passion, however purposeless that passion may seem. Because its apprehension of the "moment of sensation" is so exquisite, we rejoice in, rather than deplore, the fact that these moments have no before or after of which we can have certain knowledge. This is why *Pelléas et Mélisande,* offering what would seem to be a gloomy view of human destiny, is not in the least a depressing work, any more than are the moments of sensation which the impressionist painters discovered in their seismographic response to the visible world. These painters anarchically inverted traditional "architectural" values, made backgrounds foregrounds, allowed sitters to look outside and beyond the composition's frame, and accepted the disorder of the flux of appearances with the apparent passivity of the camera. Yet in both the painting of Monet and Degas (to choose one painter concerned mainly with the natural world and one concerned mainly with people) and in the music of Debussy the *acceptance* of Nature's disorder becomes itself a kind of order. Both find *light* within the mist of uncertainty, and something like happiness from their humility before the natural world and from their admission of human limitation. This may be why *Pelléas et Mélisande* has more to offer than its numerous progeny, which include existentialist drama, the Theater of the Absurd, and much of the music of avant-garde which we shall be discussing later in this book.

IV

The Ego and Things, and the Return to Magic: A Theme in Satie, Stravinsky and Orff

A direct link between Debussy's moment of sensation—his compassionate purposelessness—and the surrealistic cult of the irrational was provided, contemporaneously, in the music of Debussy's friend, Erik Satie. *Tristan* and *Parsifal* had brought humanism full circle, achieving religious ecstasy from the identification of Love and Death; *Pelléas et Mélisande,* dealing with the same theme, had replaced religious ecstasy with a tender fortitude. But what was the artist to do if he wasn't, like Wagner, heroic or bumptious enough to offer his inner life as a symbol of the future destiny of man, nor yet, like Debussy, courageous enough to accept the impermanence of his senses as the only truth, the only order, apprehensible to him? If he was not religious but was uncompromisingly honest, committed to the world in which he found himself, he had no choice but humbly to accept the world of appearances. He must try neither to dominate through the assertion of personality, nor to submit passively to sensation, and if human experience failed him, he must seek the logic of geometry.

In the first phase of his career—which was contemporary with *Pelléas*—Satie sought to reintegrate the disintegrated materials of tradition by juxtaposing fragments of melody and chord successions in patterns unrelated to orthodox ideas of "development." The harmonies in his Rose-Croix works are Wagnerian and Debussyan, but they differ from Wagner's harmonies in that they neither achieve nor seek any climax, and from Debussy's in that their "purposeless" oscillations accompany melodic lines that are clearly defined and exquisitely shaped. These melodic phrases are derived from plainsong, not because of its mystical associations, but because plainsong is linear, nonharmonic, impersonal and ritualistic. Satie's *Messe des Pauvres,* and all his early Rose-Croix works and piano dances, are thus "poor men's masses" in a strict and oddly touching sense. The chaste, hypnotically repeated, often pentatonic melodic phrases suggest liturgical ritual, while the wandering, rootless harmonies suggest a sensuous humanism that is lost and disembodied. The verbal irony that Satie sometimes introduced into his written directions is self-protective, and this remains true when, in the second phase of his career, he related his melodic pattern-making not to liturgical chant, but to the clichés of popular music. Since this music was communal and mechanistic, Satie found in it a musical "myth" appropriate to the antimystical world he lived in. No less than plainsong, popular music was, for Satie, impersonal and nonsubjective. So there is no *volte-face* between his first phase and his second, nor between that and his third phase wherein (especially in *Socrate* and the piano *Nocturnes*) he relinquished irony and went as far as is humanly possible—and perhaps a bit further—toward losing the personality in the pattern. In all his music, the juxtaposition of unrelated melodic and harmonic conventions induces a sense of incongruity which, like the crazy logic of *Alice in Wonderland,* is the more telling because it is self-consistent. Satie's music is childlike only in the sense that it is unusually direct, independent of the accumulations of sentiment. It moves toward the liberation of the post-Renaissance Ego from memory and desire; it is not surprising, therefore, that Satie and Debussy are among the few relatively "orthodox" composers admired by John Cage and the more advanced avant-garde.

It is obvious that Satie's attempt to reintegrate with geometric logic the splintered fragments of the past has something in common with the cubist painter's search for a geometric order beneath the broken fragments of the visible world. In addition, Satie's art was always closely associated with the ballet. In its sixteenth- and seventeenth-century origins, ballet had been a ritual of humanism, a symbolic manifestation of the belief, or wishful thought, that man could create paradise on earth. As the paradoxes inherent in humanism became more obtrusive, however, ballet either grew up into opera, which was concerned with musical and dramatic conflict and with the realities that make paradise humanly unattainable, or it became a dream-art dealing (as do Tchaikovsky's fairy-tale ballets) with the fulfillment of personal frustrations in a voiceless, timeless world of mime. Tchaikovsky's ballets are "romantic" in the sense that their world of exquisite lucidity and grace is directly related to the chaos of his own neuroses. But the "order" of balletic movement could easily become opposed to romantic introspection: a self-conscious and sophisticated ritual, as a twentieth-century ritual is bound to be. This, as we shall see, is why ballet became the favored medium of the most representative twentieth-century composer, Stravinsky; and it is also why Satie's first full-length ballet, *Parade*—created by the Diaghilev Company in 1916, to a book by Jean Cocteau, choreography by Massine, and costumes by Picasso—is a key work of our time.

Parade is a ritual which is also a dream; that is, it has no relationship to a belief or to a community, only to the images which our subconscious throws up in sleep. The action takes place in a Fair, or rather at the parade just outside the Fair, for in our spiritual isolation we are spectators at, not participators in, the dream that is life. The human beings are the circus performers, but what they do, or are made to do, bears only an illusory relationship to the dreams by which they live, which would seem to be dreams within a dream. The performers thus have the melancholy of Picasso's harlequins; even their desires are disembodied, and all that is, or seems to be, "real" is the things, the objects, among which the human comedy is enacted. Cocteau symbolizes this by making the Managers, who direct the Fair, cubist abstractions—mechanical combinations of geometric forms disguised as human (or divine) beings. The curious poignancy of the conception comes from its denial both of humanism and of theocracy. The performers' humanity lies in their dreams, but they can become "real" only through accepting things, or the world of appearances. The tragedy within the comedy is that the public (which is also the spectators in the theater, you and I) remains equally indifferent to the performers and to the Managers. They have neither human aspiration nor respect for divine authority; and perhaps they have lost aspiration because they can't be expected to show respect for gods who have become crazy engines, pushing the performers around in purposeless activity.

All the performers can do is to walk their respective tightropes as delicately as possible (while the managers crack their whips), keeping themselves going by little miracles of poise and balance. These little miracles are inherent in the music. It is the most cubist of Satie's compositions, in that each single movement, and the sequence of movements as a whole, is built on a mirror structure. Within this objective self-sufficiency are the most eccentric alliances, the most surprising contrasts of emotion. Though the music is divested of subjective intensity, a perturbing experience results from the manner in which the simplest fragments of melody and harmony are recombined in patterns that seem independent of time. These patterns are delineated by the scrupulously clean orchestration; although the ballet is scored for large forces, the instruments are treated like a chamber ensemble, and in this sense the geometric lucidity of Satie's score is a tenuously frail, yet resilient, riposte to the orchestral haze of the Debussyan unconscious. Indeed, Satie's score originally included several aural manifestations of the "real" world. Though the parts for typewriter, spinning top, revolver, sirens and tumblers, etc., were not all used in performance, they were more than the product of an unfunny dadaism. They were literally noises which, like Picasso's "objects," were to be transformed into something rich and strange.

Parade opens with an orchestral chorale, scored for brass and low strings. The effect of this is not merely, if at all, ironic. The Fair has been pitched close to a church; and humanity needs, if it forlornly cannot find, a ritual of belief. So the fugal, quasi-liturgical

"Prélude du rideau rouge" reminds us of Satie's "poor men's masses," and appropriately introduces the dream ritual of the action. After the suave but harmonically directionless ecclesiastical polyphony of this introduction we are surprised when the cubist abstraction of the French Manager appears, but the irony is pointed. The chorale has induced a "religious" mood, which the Manager appears to contradict, but doesn't, because he is the best approach we can make to a god figure.

The French Manager's theme has, indeed, already been anticipated, in solemn augmentation, in the opening chorale. Now he dances with mechanical rigidity. His tune, revolving around itself in an ambiguous rhythm that conflicts with a 3:8 ostinato swaying between E and B, suggests relentless bustle, a pointlessly ant-like energy. The theme is stated four times in various and more remorselessly nagging permutations and in increasingly harsh scoring. Its continual revolutions around an unchanging "node" and its hypnotic rhythm give it a somewhat Eastern flavor, despite its aggressiveness. So there is a natural transition when the Manager's fourth statement brings in the first of the Fairground characters—a Chinese Juggler. His Chinese getup is clearly a disguise, behind which lurks the sad smile of a Picasso or Beckett clown. Nonetheless, there is a genuinely Chinese quality, psychologically and philosophically speaking, in the nondeveloping passivity of his music. A tender delicacy, quite different from the Manager's obsessive momentum, typifies his theme. It is introduced by two flutes in swaying fifths, over a pedal F sharp on horn, like the oriental drone of eternity. The phrases are all pentatonic, the glint and clink of the ostinato patterns recognizably "Chinese" in sonority, and as he juggles with an egg, spits fire, burns his fingers and tries to put out the flames, we realize that his juggling has the pathos of human fallibility. He doesn't deal too well with the egg of birth or with the Promethean fire; Man as Hero has become the Chinese Juggler, who *just* keeps going, as well as he can. His pathos is objectified in the tenderness of a fragmentary little phrase, played first on solo horn, then on flute, that floats into the equilibrium of his nondeveloping ostinati. This tune tries to establish the serenity of the major triad, but the texture of the music gradually disintegrates until nothing is left but silence. The French Manager (thinking, no doubt, of financial loss) stamps his disgust at the public's indifference to the Juggler's display. The various fragments of the Juggler's music are played rapidly in reverse order (a musical synonym for purposelessness, for everything returns to its original form), and the Second Manager, who has been listening sympathetically to the First Manager's complaints, begins to bellow, through a megaphone, the praises of the second act.

The Second Manager is a cubist abstraction of the New World, symbolized in skyscraper forms and cowboy boots. His act is an American girl dancer, who goes through a series of actions in bewilderingly rapid sequence. She mounts a racehorse, rides a bicycle, quivers like the pictures on a cinema screen, imitates Charlie Chaplin, chases a thief with a revolver, dances a ragtime, is shipwrecked, and so on. In this hectic existence she lives her cinematic dream, the unreality of which is suggested by three distinct musical processes: the shimmering bitonal ostinato to which she first appears; the descending major thirds in her first tune, which create a whole-tone ambiguity; and the persistent syncopation which disrupts metrical regularity. The ostinato figures and whole-tone sequences tell us that her myth of fevered activity, hardly less than the Juggler's egg-balancing and fire-eating, is activity to no end. The nostalgia within her gaiety becomes patent in her ragtime dance, marked "triste." Though the static ostinati characteristic of the Juggler's music have disappeared in favor of a more sustained melody and a singing bass line, the tune has an almost chorale-like gravity; the melancholy of its symmetrical contours is enhanced by the accompanying brass chords.

Again the music disintegrates into silence. The two managers express their rage at the public's indifference in a dance *without music,* and there is a rapid recapitulation of the American girl's tunes in reverse order. The Third Manager enters: not a cubist abstraction, this time, but a dummy Negro riding a horse of unusual sagacity and aplomb. The horse—not the Negro—introduces the third act, a pair of acrobats. The young man and girl dance a fast waltz, the mechanical rhythm being picked out by xylophone. Their acrobatics are in cross-rhythm against the waltz, and the pentatonic nature of their tune and the regularity of their ostinato pattern relate them to the orientalism of the Juggler. The tenderness of their phrases contrasts with the angularity of the rhythm; they walk their tightrope precariously, hopefully emulating the flight of birds. The personnel of *Parade*—jugglers, bicycling dancers, acrobats—strikingly anticipate the unheroes of Samuel Beckett for whom (as Marshall McLuhan has pointed out) the bicycle is "the prime symbol of the Cartesian mind in its acrobatic relation of mind and body in precarious imbalance. . . . The acrobat acts as a specialist, using only a limited segment of his faculties. The clown is the integral man who mimes the acrobat in an elaborate drama of incompetence. Beckett sees the bicycle as the sign and symbol of specialist futility in the present electronic age, when we must all interact and react, using all our faculties at once."

But if Satie's acrobat lovers are (unlike the birds) the victims of fate, so apparently are the managers who seem to be controlling them. This identity of the drivers and the driven—anticipatory of the relationship between Pozzo and Lucky in *Waiting for Godot*—is musically manifest when Satie introduces an aggressive pedal on a low E, the Manager's original ostinato note. Played on an organ 32-foot stop, this causes a horrifying reverberation, over which sound rigid patterns of pentatonic fourths and sevenths. This leads once more to a recapitulation of the acrobats' material in reverse order, and so again to silence.

The organ pedal, as the voice of God, or the First Cause, scares everyone, the Managers included. The managers return *with* the various performers, and dance to a fierce orchestral tutti wherein their original "obsessive" theme is punctuated by siren blasts on the drone note, reminding us of the organ reverberation. The Chinaman, the American girl and the Acrobats leave the theater in tremulous tearfulness at the audience's lack of appreciation. The managers and the horse dance themselves into a state of collapse in their efforts to explain that the real show is still to take place inside the booth. There is an extraordinary, minatory venom in the contrast between the nagging of the Managers' self-enclosed theme and the hubbub of the tutti. The ballet ends on this note of tragic misunderstanding. The audience refuses to realize that it has seen only the "trailer" to the show, not the show itself, and the curtain falls to a telescoped version of the original fugal exposition.

In *Parade* both the spiritual rhythm and the corporeal rhythm have submitted to geometry, and the pathos of Satie's circus performers consists in the passive inarticulateness with which they keep going, even though there seems to be no point in it beyond the geometry of the abstract patterns they make. But although they are inarticulate, they don't totally surrender their humanity in accepting a mechanistic, post-Cartesian world which would equate them with inanimate things. If in one sense a denial of life, they are also a point from which new growth may begin.

"Je suis venu au monde très jeune," Satie said, "dans un temps très vieux." The probity and the intrinsic beauty of his compositions are his only necessary justification: which cannot finally be separated from those quasi-philosophical gestures which have made him a John the Baptist to the mid-twentieth-century avant-garde. In his *musique d'ameublement* he invented the pre-juke box Musak which is anti-art in that it is not meant to be listened to; while in remarking that "this work is utterly incomprehensible, even to me," or that "experience is one of the forms of paralysis," he came close to the complete acceptance of purposelessness as a *principle,* which is typical of Cage and Beckett. Like them, he combines provocation with boredom (his *Vexations* is an eighty-second piece which is to be played 840 times!); like them, he knew that "boredom is mysterious and profound." Even in the purely musical aspects of his work, however, Satie negates European history. Although his basic fragmented materials are all—except possibly in the early *Gnossiennes*—Western, his static approach to the time sense and the syllabic rhythmic structure of his later music, especially *Socrate,* have much in common with the numerical rhythms of John Cage; and how deep this orientalism runs is suggested by the tiny piano pieces called *Sports et Divertissements,* written in 1914. Seldom more than two or three lines long, they are copied in colored inks in Satie's exquisite musical hand, accompanied by a verbal commentary, which is meant to be looked at, not recited; they must be almost unique in European art in depending, like Japanese haiku, simultaneously on music, poetry and calligraphy.

Gertrude Stein—who greatly admired Satie, and whose linguistic patterns have affinities with Satie's sound patterns—perceived how the cult of the object or "thing" leads to the rediscovery of the child, and how that is linked to the rediscovery of primitive instinct and of non-Western cultures. Speaking of two greater artists, Stravinsky and Picasso, who are closely related both to Satie and to herself, she said:

> And then it came to me it is perfectly simple, the Russian and Spaniard are Oriental, and there is the same mixture. Scratch a Russian and you find a Tartar. Scratch a Spaniard and you find a Saracen. And all this is very important with what I have been saying about the peaceful Oriental penetration into European culture or rather the tendency for this generation that is for the twentieth century to be no longer European perhaps because Europe is finished.*

We have discussed the sense in which, in the music of Schoenberg and Debussy, "Europe is finished," and have commented on Schoenberg's frustrated search for a renewal of spirit. Complementary to Schoenberg's attempt, however, man had to seek the body's renewal, and this search too involved a turning away from "Europe." This is evident in the "Russian" works with which Stravinsky—the third, central, key figure in twentieth-century music—opened his long career.

It is instructive to compare Stravinsky's ballet *Petrouchka,* also written for Diaghilev, with Satie's *Parade.* That there is something in common between the two works is obvious, for the circus performers in *Parade* are puppet-like and (in Picasso's decor and costumes) have some relationship to commedia dell'arte characters, while Stravinsky's characters are ostensibly puppets and Petrouchka himself is a Russian fairy-tale version of Pierrot. Just as the circus performers in *Parade* are controlled, or seem to be controlled, by

* Gertrude Stein, *Everybody's Autobiography* (London: 1938).

the managers, so the puppets in *Petrouchka* are activated by a Showman, significantly also titled the Charlatan, whose role as synthetic god figure is suggested by his portrait painted on a back-cloth; wearing sumptuous apparel, he squats on a cloud, like a baroque *deus ex machina.* There are also many technical features in common between the two ballets, for *Petrouchka,* like *Parade,* depends on very short melodic phrases incantatorily repeated in geometric patterns, on recurrent ostinati, on nondeveloping oscillations between chords and on surprising juxtapositions of mood (reflecting the multifarious bustle of the Fair). The difference between the two works—which is no less remarkable than the similarity—derives from the Russian origins of Stravinsky's music, which gives it a corporeal energy that Satie's music does not have. This means that its "documentary" significance is less uncompromising than Satie's work, while its human potentiality is higher. But it isn't, in this piece, much more than potentiality. Whether or not Stravinsky was aware of this, we may see *Petrouchka* as a parable of the sickness of our century, from an awareness of which all Stravinsky's later work developed.

Thus the Russian peasant world, in which the Fair takes place in *Petrouchka,* is a real world, whereas *Parade* takes place in a no man's land *outside* the Fair. Yet Petrouchka-Pierrot—who is Modern Man no less than Schoenberg's Pierrot Lunaire, Debussy's Pierrot *fâché avec la lune,* or Picasso's harlequins—is, as puppet and artist, shut out from this world, and the parable concerns his struggle toward a Western, unpeasant-like "consciousness." His story is a comic, Chaplinesque tragedy: he loves the ballerina, Columbine, who is the sophisticated Western world in decay (she dances to a Russianized permutation of a Lanner waltz that came from Vienna, the melting pot of Europe), and he is destroyed by a Moor, who is the primitive and bestial roots of our natures, whose music is both savage and sumptuous, orgiastic and oriental. The Ballerina's civilization and the Moor's animality ought to be complementary virtues, but she is a heartless chit of a girl and he is a stupid oaf who falls down to worship a coconut; so when their two tunes are played together as they dance, the effect is of grim farce.

That this breakdown, this dislocation between Nature and Nurture, is peculiarly a product of twentieth-century stresses is suggested in the last act. A peasant enters driving a dancing bear on a chain, to a hurdy-gurdy tune that revolves obsessively around itself; the bear is related to Petrouchka's struggle to aspire from puppetdom to consciousness. A Rich Man distributes banknotes indiscriminately to the crowd who, if ostensibly human, seem to be no less automatic in their movements than the Moor and the Ballerina, and much more so than Petrouchka. A rout of Masquers comes in accompanied by Devil, Goat (lust), and Pig (greed and stupidity), emphasizing the theme of Appearance and Reality. The Devil, his theme leaping through sevenths and ninths on the brass, excites the crowd to savage, nonhuman hysteria. It is at this point that cries are heard from the puppet theater and Petrouchka rushes out pursued by the Moor, who kills him because he had attempted to rescue the Ballerina from the Blackamoor's ravishment. The crowd, despite its exuberance, is hardly more aware of suffering, or of any kind of feeling, than is the audience in *Parade*. *Petrouchka* is, however, slightly less pessimistic than *Parade,* because after the crowd has slowly dispersed to accordion harmonies that run down like a melancholy clock, the puppet-Pierrot is not, after all, finally deflated. The sawdust seems to be pouring out of him; as the Charlatan points out, he was only a puppet, so his murder is of no consequence. Yet the puppet-artist turns out to be more "real" than the crowd, just as the cubist abstractions in *Parade* were more real than the audience. It seems that he has a soul. His ghost appears above the little theater-within-a-theater, jeering at the Showman, who nervously drops the body and scuttles off, to a snarl of bitonal trumpets based on the F-sharp major–C-major tritonal tension that had originally expressed Petrouchka's—and the artist's—separation from an insensate world. This whimpering flicker of "consciousness" suggests how, for Stravinsky, *Petrouchka* was a starting point, not an end. The first stage in his pilgrimage toward the puppet's regeneration into man was to begin *ab ovo:* to learn to accept the Blackamoor's bestiality as in itself potentially a virtue.

This happens in the series of pseudoprimitive works that succeeds *Petrouchka.*

Thus Stravinsky's *The Rite of Spring* is both a fertility ritual and a sacrificial act, like Schoenberg's "Dance Around the Golden Calf." Unlike Schoenberg's work, however, it exists as an end in itself, not as a negation of something else, and this is true even though it contains within itself both a destructive and a reconstructive principle. Superficially, its primitivism may seem to be destructive, associated with the sadistic violence that was ravaging Europe in the first of the World Wars. But it is also constructive, in so far as it returns to the roots of human experience, suggesting that if consciousness has led civilization to this pass, we'd do well to be rid of it, at least temporarily. The instinctual experience of primitive peoples, who surrendered their egoism in a communal act, was at least genuine, without emotional prevarication. *The Rite of Spring* attempts to re-enter, to re-create, a primitive ritual of death and creation. Of course, it cannot do so; if we experience the ballet in a theater we know that we are not in fact taking part in a ritual murder, but are only being self-consciously unself-conscious, deliberately liberating the libido. This may be good for us, and was certainly a necessary step for Stravinsky. Using the stylized gestures of ballet mime and the sophisticated paraphernalia of an enormous symphony orchestra, he explored one of the sources of strength which he, as a Russian, possessed, and which modern, "Western" man had surrendered. It was not something about which Western man could be indifferent, though he might, as the scenes at the notorious first performance testify, be scared to the point of hysteria. At this date we can see, or rather hear, how the "destructive" sadism of *The Rite of Spring* leads inevitably into its spring-like renewal. Though still immensely exciting, it is no longer frightening, as Schoenberg's "Dance" is and, in the context of the opera as a whole, always will and should be.

We can also see now that although the music of Stravinsky's rite is violent, whereas Debussy's music is usually nonviolent, the two are closely related both technically and "philosophically." Both use short, hypnotic melodic phrases, often pentatonic, in incantatory repetition, and both employ a static harmonic texture which, involving oscillations between chords and recurrent ostinati, produces an effect more oriental than occidental. Stravinsky's rhythms are corporeally energetic, whereas Debussy's are passive or nonexistent; yet since these rhythms are hypnotically repetitive, they, too, tend to destroy the temporal sense and on occasion to break into complex, additive, ecstasy-inducing meters comparable with those found in real primitive music. Moreover, Stravinsky, in using the orchestra as a gigantic percussion instrument that deprives the individual instruments of melodic and harmonic identity, creates an effect comparable with Debussy's atmospheric "cocoon" of sound. This is true of the rowdily orgiastic passages as well as of the nocturnal interludes, such as the strange and marvelous piece that introduces the dance of the adolescent girls. Stravinsky's use of incremental rondo form in the final "Sacrificial Dance" is also related both to the incantatory repetition of primitive music and to the nondeveloping processes of Debussy.

The Rite of Spring is a "sport" in Stravinsky's career which could be done once only. Its release, both of violence and of potency, profoundly influenced his later work however, and through that, the whole of Western music. The transition is effected in *The Wedding,* which Stravinsky sets not in a primeval past, but in a Russian peasant world that, although immensely ancient in its traditions, probably still existed when the work was composed. (It is interesting that although all the tunes sound folk-like, there is only one authentic folk tune in the score, and that is a modern factory song.) This means that the life ritual has a more immediate reality than it had in *The Rite,* especially since we no longer have ritual murders, but do have weddings, which are at once a personal act, a social act, and a ritual of creation. Stravinsky intended this dual relationship to past and present to be manifest in the performance; the dancers were to use stylized forms of genuine peasant rituals, but the musicians were to be visible on the stage, in modern evening dress. This would suggest that, although "true," the ritual was also a masquerade in which we are involved, but only vicariously. This wasn't in fact done in performance, though a somewhat similar effect was achieved by making the dance movements in part geometrical and architectural, with stylized black and white costumes and decor. For us uprooted creatures the "cubist" abstraction of *Parade* is unavoidable, for we are to some degree *abstracted* from experience. Here, however, in the dance ceremony, is an ideal of emotional and physical spontaneity which is still real, and which we can share to some degree, because we still know something, however little, about falling in love, and desire or lust, and family ties, and fear and parting. The realism of *The Wedding* extends to the scoring. Stravinsky abandons the gigantic symphony orchestra of *The Rite,* which is inescapably associated with European "concert" music, in favor of a percussion band wherein four pianos emulate the sounds of genuine peasant bands (he had originally intended to use "local" instruments, such as the cymbalon). Moreover, he introduces voices, singing, speaking and shouting in pentatonic phrases which are close to the origins of song in speech or yell. Words and human voices bring in "reality," as they do in the operas of Tchaikovsky, as compared with the silent mime of his ballets. However, Stravinsky places his singers in the orchestra, so that the reality of the experience is deliberately separated from the miming of it by the dancers.

The musical technique carries that of *The Rite of Spring* to a more extreme point. The post-Renaissance element of "personal" expression is almost completely denied, for there is no melody except brief ostinato utterances, no harmony, and virtually no modulation. The music depends entirely on the "melodic tonality" of incantatory phrases oscillating around a nodal point; on hypnotic patterns of rhythm, beginning corporeally, but becoming "additive" at points of maximum excitement; and on percussive dissonance. This latter element is sophisticated by the use of unresolved appoggiaturas, which emphasize the barbarism while giving it an edge of hysteria which may be modern rather than primitive. Bartók uses a similar technique in the percussive works of his "middle" period.

Whereas *The Rite* is entirely pagan, *The Wedding* fuses pagan with Christian ritual, as does the Russian peasant society in which it happens. This more "modern" feature is reflected in the fact that the wedding is both a communal celebration and fertility rite, and also something that concerns a specific pair of human creatures. They have solo parts, while the chorus represent the community. This duality is established in the first scene, the "Benediction of the Bride." The people, dressing her hair, sing in fierce, unflinching ostinati, oscillating around the node E. She has the same notes but in transposed octaves, so that she utters a cry of personal pain. This is both physical (for they are tugging her hair) and nervous (for she is scared of the unknown). They try to console her, in a more lyrical phrase, hypnotically repeated. This phrase is in the other pentatonic scale on E, with an A-ish feeling, accompanied by less harsh percussion noises, rather like a Balinese gamelan. These noises continue while they describe the garden of Love where the nightingale sings, but ostinato dissonances obtrude percussively into the pentatonicism, in contrary motion polytonal triads, because her lover's approach will wake her up. Repeated E's rise almost to hysteria and carry us back to the "tressing" motive. She sings a lovely, lyrical pentatonic phrase about her blue ribbon, while they continue their sadistic ululations, imitating her tune (perhaps parodistically) on occasion. She ends in wistfulness, her phrase declining as she says the ribbon is blue, like her eyes.

This benediction, in which all the tunes are based on the pentatonic minor third and major second, has been mainly pagan. The second tableau, the "Benediction of the Bridegroom," is specifically Christian, though the technique is unchanged. We begin with male voices intoning metrically repeated notes, with no hint of the pentatonic lyricism, around a new nodal point, C. The parents are here to some degree characterized, or perhaps caricatured, for they are not presented, as the lovers are, as potential human consciousness. They sing folk-like incantations, with oriental-sounding chromaticisms, to convey their anguish at the thought that "another will love them." But the chorus community brushes aside this personal feeling in asking for the benediction of the saints on the marriage, in quick, rhythmic intonation. The Bridegroom himself asks for his parents' blessing and the general benediction becomes orgiastic over a double ostinato. The next tableau performs the same function for the Bride, whose parents are also characterized, as she leaves home to regular rhythmic ostinati, and to the lyrical A-ish version of the nondeveloping pentatonic tune. Polytonal triads in contrary motion work up the excitement as everyone goes out; the two mothers indulge together in a little chromatic whimper of self-pity, mincing and wheezing around the nodal point A.

The final tableau is the marriage feast, scored for double chorus (the two families) with all the percussion in action. Although still built around nodal ostinati, the music now employs a number of different nodes simultaneously, so that the bustle is increased. Sundry village characters look in on the festivities, interrupting from various parts of the chorus. The lovers are brought together by the two families and instructed about their domestic duties. Suddenly the racket stops and the girl sings solo, "I was far away on a great sea": a more expansive lyrical tune built on rising fourths. The chorus embraces the fourths in a rocking lullaby, comparing the lovers to Leda and the Swan. This introduces the "moment of love" and the bed-warming; the chorus, beginning tenderly with pentatonic patterns around the node E, grows gradually fiercer and more sharply dissonant, returning to its social role as the japes and bawdy jokes increase outside the bedroom door. The song becomes half speech here, for everyone is tipsy. But when the lover has gone in to his love, the clatter-chatter stops, and he sings the only continuous cantilena in the work. This is a sublimation of the melodic ideas of the whole piece, still pentatonic but flowing and growing, both a personal and a social fulfillment. It is unaccompanied except for static gong and bell noises around B—the *dominant* of the original node E. So this love song is, like the Song of Songs, at once sensual and religious; love makes the fragments of physical energy and sensation grow into song, which is a monodic outpouring of Spirit. The relationship between song and speech in Schoenberg's *Moses and Aaron* is thus reversed. The bells and gongs get slower and slower until we're left with the moment of love's consummation in the silence of the night, and the physical consummation is a revelation of Spirit. This miraculous freeing of song from the burden of Self, this obliteration of Time, is a deeply moving musical synonym for re-creation; if it seems to be a denial of the Western world, this denial was essential for Stravinsky if, in his later work, the Christian religious consciousness was to be reborn.

Nor is it entirely just to say that this re-created primitivism, this liberation of the corporeal into the spiritual, is *merely* a stage which Stravinsky himself passed through. For it has had repercussions in other and later composers and, as we shall see, ultimately links up with the other "retreat from Europe" that began, not as a reassertion, but as a denial of corporeality. Even before this fusion is effected we can observe, in the music of Carl Orff, an example of the survival value of Stravinskian primitivism. We may think, and would be justified in thinking, that Orff is a small composer compared with Stravinsky. But if he has concentrated only on one aspect of Stravinsky's work and hasn't "grown to consciousness" with the European-Russian, it is not true to say that he has left Stravinsky's primitive phase exactly where he found it, that he has done nothing, in thirty years of music creation, except repeat what Stravinsky had already done better. Though we have often been encouraged to think of *Carmina Burana*—the work with which Orff made his name—as a poor man's *Les Noces,* the analogy has no more than limited validity. It is obvious that Orff's work is restricted in rhythmic and textural invention compared with Stravinsky's masterpiece; it should be equally obvious that Orff's work has certain assets which are outside Stravinsky's range. Quite simply, what Orff has is "the gift to be simple," as the old Shaker song puts it: a gift of memorably haunting tunefulness, exemplified, for instance, in the soprano solos from the Court of Love movement; and those who think such tunefulness is easy should try it. The medieval Latin and Middle German texts are pre-Renaissance, halfway between Christian "consciousness" and a direct, immediate ("pagan") acceptance of life in and for the senses. While some vestiges of traditional harmonic practice remain, this music, flowering from the dawn of Europe, expresses itself mainly through rhythmic excitation and through melodies that are in essence physical gestures: there is no dichotomy between thought and process, and emotion becomes the body's action, which is meant—as in all Orff's works—to be physically projected on a stage. So this music, with its beguiling tunefulness and the patterned symmetry of its rhythms, is a ritual related to the innocence of real folk music, to the street songs and runes of childhood itself, and to contemporary pop, which has at its heart an adolescent yearning for release from self-consciousness. Certainly *Carmina Burana* may have some historical significance as a genuine halfway house between concert music and pop. Like the tunes and rhythms of the Beatles, its banality is sometimes inspired; and this may be salutary, even though it doesn't invalidate the adult experience of greater composers.

Stravinsky's primitivism is merely one tensely ambiguous aspect of his response to the contemporary scene; with Orff we really are born again into childhood. That this return might be a new start in a different sense from Stravinsky's recreation of the past is suggested by a comparison of Stravinsky's *Wedding* with Orff's *Trionfo di Afrodite* of 1950. Both pieces describe a nuptial ceremony; but Orff's wedding carries on where Stravinsky's leaves off, in that the elements of corporeal rhythm and of melismatic monodic lyricism are now equally weighted. Orff's piece, like Stravinsky's, is a "concerto scenico" for solo voices representing the lovers and for chorus representing the people. It is accompanied by an orchestra in which normal forces are used abnormally, reinforced by a very large percussion battery. The music is meant to flow into action, mimed by dancers on a stage. It is significant that the texts, taken from Catullus, Sappho and Euripedes, and sung in the original Greek and Latin, have none of the Christian associations from which Stravinsky's return to European consciousness was to spring; they are a restatement of elemental pagan truths which Orff believes to be eternal. Though the essence of the music is sensual and corporeal, Orff is justified in saying that in his ritual of marriage and fertility "the timely element disappears" and "spiritual power" is generated from physical action. This is manifest, naturally, in the technique of the music itself. The structure of the seven sections of the work is dramatically comparable with that of Stravinsky's *The Wedding;* we begin with a "Song of the Maidens and Youth to the Evening Star," while awaiting the Bride and Bridegroom, and proceed to a wedding procession, a meeting of the Bride and Bridegroom, an invocation and "Hymn to Hymen," and to nuptial games and songs before the lovers are led into the Wedding Chamber. We don't, however, have to wait for the ultimate consummation and the epilogic appearance of Aphrodite for the translation of corporeality into spirit, for the two elements are in equipoise throughout. Thus, the percussive ostinati are simpler than in Stravinsky, even when excitement is enhanced by cross-rhythms. As a result, the rhythmic patterns can carry simple melodic phrases which, though still incantatory and hypnotic, are more lyrical than Stravinsky's, and in that sense more fulfilled in their innocence. Similarly, the ostinati of diatonic harmonies are more consonant, less exacerbated by unresolved percussive dissonances than Stravinsky's, while the more varied colors of the orchestra, used ritualistically rather than atmospherically, attain a glowing incandescence. Choirs of brass and woodwind, interspersed with the homophonic vocal choirs, give the percussive noises of bells, gongs, pianos and drums a simple melodic and harmonic identity, whereas in Stravinsky percussive attributes communicate themselves to the melodic and harmonic instruments. So, even in the opening movement, the metrically chanted incantations to Hymen can be interrupted by solo voice invocations to the Evening Star, wherein all physical movement, and even the most rudimentary harmony, stop, and the voices sing whirling melismata over a static drone. In these stepwise-moving, "spiritually" rhythmed melismata, from which temporal accents have vanished, the pentatonic love song such as concludes Stravinsky's *The Wedding* flowers and burgeons. And in the beautiful third movement, when the Bride and Bridegroom meet, we have an extended section of music which is entirely lyrical cantilena over a drone. This music is certainly more oriental than occidental in technique and feeling, while carrying conviction within this twentieth-century work. Thus the finale—the consummation of the marriage itself—does not (like the conclusion of Stravinsky's piece) carry us into a *different,* more spiritual world; rather, it consummates the identity of flesh and spirit of which we are already aware, just as, in real primitive ritual, erotic orgy would lead without break into religious ceremonial, and *vice versa.*

It is significant that the "Song before the Wedding Chamber" is the most *songful* of all the incantatory chants, though it still has a hypnotic pattern and an undeviating metrical pulse. Beginning quietly and tenderly, it rises to orgiastic fervor, and leads into the scene in the Wedding Chamber when the Bride and Bridegroom make love in entirely nonharmonic, nonmetrical melismatic lyricism, monodically unaccompanied, or with the simplest sustained drone. Their pentatonicism turns into rising chromatics as they twine together in sensuous parallel thirds, and the melismata of their ultimate love cries is the music most completely liberated from metrical Time and from the earth pull of harmony. So the final invocation of Aphrodite is an inevitable sequel to the physical consummation, which musically as well as dramatically had been presaged in the third scene when the Bride and Bridegroom had been awakened, by the lyre's music, to the spiritual reality of their love.

One can easily say—and it is true—that the music of this *Trionfo di Afrodite* is extraordinarily simple, even childish, to have been created in the mid-twentieth century. Yet if the music convinces, its simplicity is its strength, and its childishness a positive virtue. It links up with the music Orff has composed especially for children, because he believes that any renewal within modern civilization must grow from the young, who alone preserve some notion of the instinctive celebration that art once was. Orff's *Trionfo* may be an odd piece to have been written in our time. Nonetheless, the fact that it *has* been written is important, and although it's unlikely that many composers will either want or be able to compose similar music, it reminds us of certain positive values that will have to be preserved, or reborn, in any vital music of the future. It is a *positive* answer to Schoenberg's "Dance Around the Golden Calf," and the fact that Schoenberg's dance is a greater as well as more complex piece of music does not alter the fact that some such answer was necessary. That Orff's primitivism is not merely regressive is indicated if we consider him in relation to Olivier Messiaen who, as one of the shapers of the "New Music," learned much from both the serial and the Debussyan revolution.

V

The Circle Renewed: The "New Music" from Messiaen to Berio

We have seen that Schoenberg's tussle with the flesh, beginning with the Tristanesque *Verklärte Nacht,* led to a desperate search for a rebirth of spirit, and that Debussy sought a renewal of the spiritual simply by accepting the sensory moment as an end in itself. No less pagan in outlook, Orff and the early Stravinsky were composers whose rediscovery of corporeality led to a recreation of the irrational, the magically intuitive, which (in Stravinsky's case at least) was to lead to a renewal within Christian consciousness itself. Olivier Messiaen, on the other hand, was born within Christian tradition, while being no less passionate, sensuous and even paganly erotic in sensibility than Debussy, his compatriot and forebear. Of its nature his music is far more highly charged, harmonically, than that of the ritualists Orff and Stravinsky. In this sense it is more nervously personal, less communal; yet even in his earliest, most sensuous works it was evident that his harmonically centered music could tend toward ritual, in that he carried the isolation of the sensory moment from before and after to a still more extreme point than did Debussy. Indeed, the more highly charged are the artist's sensations, the greater is the need to be released from the grip of the Will. So the movement of the chromatic chords in a piece like *Le Banquet Céleste* is so slow as to be almost stationary, and the chords are so submerged in a plethora of "added notes" as to be without tonal identity; similarly, the relationships between the chords are as disturbingly without harmonic *direction* as are the comparable passages in the Rose-Croix pieces of Erik Satie. The later, immense piano work *Vingt Regards sur l'Enfant Jésus* is a series of "looks" in that each movement is virtually without movement, being built on an alternation of two or three chords, an ostinato, a pedal note and a reiterated figuration. This, again, is a vast expansion of the static technique explored in tiny works by Satie, and implicit in the "spatial" aspects of Debussy's music. Since such music evades the concept of beginning, middle and end, the European time-sense is no longer relevant to it. This is why Messiaen's works last, chronometrically speaking, so long. There is no reason why they—any more than a Gothic motet or the improvisation of an Indian vina player—should ever stop.

The combination of these spatial and ritualistic techniques with such sumptuous and nervously titillating harmony suggests that Messiaen's music started from a desire to sublimate his eroticism comparable to that of another fervent Roman Catholic, César Franck (who was also an organist, at times drunk with the sensory power that the organ, being a one-man band, may give to the player). Messiaen's sublimatory mysticism would seem, however, to be the more authentic, for it has specific musical consequences. Thus, whereas Franck's chromatic harmonies, trying to grow, revolve narcissistically around themselves, Messiaen's harmonies, making no pretense of growth, can proliferate (like Debussy's) into melodic arabesques related to medieval cantillation. The cult of Mariolatry in Messiaen's music may be directly related to the Mariolatry of the original troubadours, for whom the Eternal Beloved was at once the Virgin Mary and an earth goddess. We remember that for the Gnostics Jesus was conceived of a Holy Spirit (which was female in Hebrew) moving "on the face of the waters," and that the name of the mother in whom he was made flesh originally meant "of the sea." So the Virgin Mary cannot have been so far removed from Aphrodite, "the Wise One of the Sea," from whom descended Eleusis the Divine Child—after whom the Eleusinian Mysteries were named. The "return to the waters of the unconscious" is thus implicit in Messiaen's Christianity, and it is not surprising that, in intuitively rediscovering the remote mythological roots of his religion, he should metamorphose Christian chastity into fecundity, in a whirl of ornament both linear and harmonic. This may also be why, in later works, medieval Christian features merge into a conception that is ritualistic in a more general sense, and the neomedieval techniques become inseparable from oriental processes. Not only does Messiaen employ Eastern melismatic devices, he also uses Indian ragas and talas both in pure and in modified form. Sometimes the chord formations may be a vertical statement of a traditional or invented raga; sometimes the themes may be a horizontal version of the "mystic chords," a procedure close to that of Scriabin, a still more esoteric musical theosophist who, depriving sensual harmonies of momentum, aimed to create a Mystery, performed in a hemispherical temple in India, which would induce in the participants a "supreme final ecstasy," after which the physical plane of consciousness would dissolve away and a world cataclysm begin.

Belonging to an orthodox church, Messiaen is less atomically literal, but it is significant that the work that sums up the first phase of his career should have been written in 1940 (in a prison camp), a year in which a catacylsm was indeed unleashed. The *Quatuor pour la fin du temps* for clarinet, violin, cello and piano relates this factual experience to the Apocalypse. Seven movements parallel the days of creation and the Day of Rest, while an eighth movement transports us to Eternity. The beautiful first movement, "Liturgie de Cristal," consists of bird twitters at dawn, in "le silence harmonieux du ciel," floating over a repeated metrical pattern or tala on the piano. The piano's chords are deprived of their Western sense of progression, while the bird song, in its numerical rhythm, is related to Eastern monody. This links Messiaen's Catholic mysticism to his pantheism, his awareness of Nature as an "other," a nonhuman reality. From this point of view there are affinities between his music and the Stravinsky of *The Rite of Spring,* as well as the obvious analogy with Debussy. In "Liturgie de Cristal" the birds are both Nature's voice and God's, and therefore are also man's desire for a heaven beyond consciousness. The destruction of

Time and consciousness is then prophesied by the Angel of the Apocalypse, who announces the consummation of the divine mystery. This movement is violent but nondeveloping: it releases the "bird" of the spirit who, in the next movement, sings alone, from the abyss of Time, in an unaccompanied clarinet arabesque. Monody and Spirit are here explicitly identified, and the arabesque technique is a fulfillment of the oriental implications of the flute solo in *Pierrot Lunaire,* for it employs not only raga and tala series and floating, additive rhythms, but also pitch distortions such as could not occur in a Western context. This liberation of the bird voice cannot be an end for Messiaen, however, for he has, after all, Europe's past behind him. This may be suggested by the brief, scherzo-like movement that follows, which seems to oppose the bird voice to the terrestrial, even trivial, circumstances of our everyday lives; the dancing, simple-textured, relatively diatonic music combines charm and grace with a faintly comic pathos. If this is our frail humanity, it leads us to the specifically Christian element of the work: the humanity that God assumed for our sake. The next movement is a cantilena for solo cello, representing Christ as the Word, accompanied by pulsing piano chords in an isochronous rhythmic pattern. Though this pattern is preordained, and in that sense medieval and possibly oriental too, the chords themselves are richly chromatic and in that sense humanistic. The long, floating cello melody flows over, and grows out of, the harmonic tensions. Identifying Christ with us, the music tells us that our sensuality, pain and mortality can find lyrical assuagement through Christ, as the notes of the melody become increasingly sustained, the pulse of Time slower and slower.

It is only after Christ's Incarnation that the Seven Trumpets of the Apocalypse can ring out. They, of course, are entirely monodic, because the divine voice (whether represented by Nature's birds or by God Himself) cannot admit the intrusion of "human" harmony. They also sound in a preordained meter, rotating in an eternal circle; here, conventional European instruments are made to create an extraordinary, gong-like, brazen sonority. When the Angel of the Apocalypse effects Time's destruction in the seventh movement, Word and Flesh become one; melismatic arabesque is absorbed into, and grows out of, a ripely sensuous piano harmony and, at times, a jazzily orgiastic and corporeal rhythm. The coda movement for violin and piano returns to earth—unlike Schoenberg's *Moses and Aaron*—to take us into heaven. Representing Christ as Man, it complements the cello solo that, representing Christ as Word, had concluded the first part of the work. Significantly, it is the fact of Incarnation that brings us our heavenly vision. The "endless" line of the solo violin floats higher and higher until, with oriental melismata, it fades away, "paradisiaque," into the stellar spaces, while the piano pulsates, with senses suspended, on high (Debussyan) chords of the added sixth. Here, as in the much simpler music of Orff, eroticism is a gateway to mysticism.

From Messiaen's later works the "humanism" inherent in the rich texture of the *Quatuor* has, for the most part, disappeared. The chords become increasingly percussive in effect, without harmonic meaning in the Western sense; complementarily, the organization depends increasingly on a kind of magical-oriental serialism. If the Christian element in these pieces is less patent, their nonhuman, pagan "magic" is no less erotic in impulse. One of the most remarkable of these works that introduce Messiaen's third phase is the *Cinq Rechants* for twelve unaccompanied voices, written in 1948, and specifically described as a "chant d'amour." In this work the division between sacred and profane has ceased to exist. As Messiaen has himself pointed out, the work has two musical sources: the Harawi, a love song from the pagan folklore of Peru and Ecuador; and the Alba, or medieval dawn song, which warns the lovers of the approaching day. The text, by Messiaen himself, is partly in surrealistic French and partly in an invented, pseudo-Hindu language that dissolves "meaning" into purely musical sound images: these sometimes become bird or insect or animal noises. References to Tristan and Isolde, Vivian and Merlin, Orpheus and other legendary lovers occur alongside contemporary references (for instance to the flying lovers in the paintings of Marc Chagall). Although the movement of the note values is almost consistently rapid, thereby suggesting "the dramatic brevity of life," the forms are all nonevolutionary and the harmonies, in so far as they exist, nonprogressive. The Beloved stands beyond Time, "ses yeux voyagent dans le passé, dans l'avenir," and the same neutral tritone symbolizes the before and the after, of which we can have no certain knowledge.

If the structures have no relationship to Western tonal development, they have close connections with oriental serial permutation and with medieval variation techniques; the title *Rechants* is borrowed from the French Renaissance composer Claude le Jeune, who experimented in numerical rhythms derived from verbal inflection. After a free, monodic invocation in the invented language, the first Rechant introduces the panoply of legendary lovers, either monodically, in wildly whirling leaps controlled by the Deci Tala pattern of 2 plus 2 plus 3/16 alternating with 2/8, or in brutal, somewhat Stravinskian homophony. Interspersing reiterations and permutations of these brief motives are more extended, lyrical couplets in two- or three-part polyphony. The texture and rhythmic patterns are here medieval, though the sound doesn't lose its tender, post-Renaissance voluptuousness, partly because of the recurrent thirds in the texture, partly because of caressing grace notes comparable with those of oriental monody. It is interesting that the words of this section describe the crystal bubble in which Hieronymus Bosch enclosed his lovers. Medievally biased, Bosch saw the encroachment of Renaissance will as a nightmare; Messiaen, at the twilight of the Renaissance, relinquishes the tonal perspective analogous to the visual perspective that Bosch had just become aware of, and once more dissolves antecedence and sequence in discontinuous space.

Each of the five Rechants is constructed on this same principle: an introductory invocation; the Rechant (which is the ritornello or refrain of troubadour music), alternating with Couplets; and a coda which returns to the original invocation and sometimes includes motives from the Rechant and Couplets also. There is no climax within the individual movements, though one might possibly say that the central (third) Rechant forms an apex to the whole work. It begins, not with strict monody, but with undulating tritonal cantilena accompanied by wordless, sensuously static chords and attains, from this sensuality, the highest degree of magical or "doctrinal" impersonality, since the three verses are in nonreversible rhythm, developed by augmentation and then by diminution of the central values. "The left and right values remain invariably symmetrical. In the third verse the effect is maintained and intensified by a long crescendo, which unfurls like a veil of sound in twelve-part canon, culminates in a collective cry, and falls back to a soft, supple, and tender coda." There is a direct affinity between this cry and the yell of consummated passion in Orff's *Afrodite,* and it may be significant that in the later Rechants tritonal figurations become increasingly prevalent in the melodic lines themselves. Indeed, the basic theme of the fourth Rechant is the *si contra fa* that used to be the Devil, and the ululation of the Couplets is all tritonal organum. The tritones from which Tristan yearned to be released seem to have become, monodically, a positive; the Flesh has become the Word. In this sense Messiaen can claim to have created, in the triptych of works of which *Cinq Rechants* is the last, a song of love and death which is a positive continuation of the Wagnerian cycle; Tristan no longer needs to die in order to achieve the metamorphosis of Flesh into Spirit. Debussy, in depriving Wagnerian harmony of the need for resolution, had shown the way to the apotheosis of the flesh; Messiaen completes the process by transforming harmonic tension into monodic line.

It would be difficult to imagine a more complete reversal of the will domination of post-Renaissance Europe than the gigantic *Turangalîla Symphony*—the second member of the triptych of love and death that concludes Messiaen's middle period. In this work the corybantic fast movements are significantly allied to the new-old primitivism of jazz both in the hypnotic repetitiveness of their riffs and breaks and in the blatantly scored juiciness of their harmony. They seem as eternally long, as Time-obliterating, as the slow movements which evoke the sensual heaven of a garden of love wherein the birds (represented by a gamelan orchestra of piano, vibraphone, xylophone and celesta) ecstatically twitter, both tonally and rhythmically independent of the almost stationary string homophony.

Such a pantheistic attempt to create a musical cosmos embracing man, God and the natural world increasingly dominates Messiaen's later works, such as *Le Reveil des Oiseaux* for piano and orchestra. In 1953 this work inaugurated the series of compositions based on the scrupulous imitation of the songs of birds. The writing here, as in the *Cinq Rechants,* tends to be monophonic in principle, even when the strings are divided in thirty-two parts! And the fascinating sonorities are an ultimate expression of Debussy's desire to "reproduce what I hear . . . the mysterious accord that exists between Nature and the human imagination." Of the quality of Messiaen's imagination —which creates out of the imitation of Nature—there can be no doubt; even so, there are times, especially in the immense and apparently interminable *Catalogues d'Oiseaux* for piano solo, when one finds oneself wondering whether Messiaen hasn't carried "l'atrophie du Moi" a bit too far. Maybe birds are angel voices that have something we have lost; nonetheless one can't completely follow Debussy in saying that there is more to be gained by watching the sun rise than by listening to the *Pastoral Symphony,* for sunrises, like birds, have never lost something that Beethoven had, because they never had it to lose. However post-Renaissance man may have misused his knowledge and his power, he certainly hasn't toiled through centuries of "the pain of consciousness" to end up listening to the birds —while squatting on an oriental midden.

Such subversive grumblings as one has permitted oneself, however, have been negated in the event. Even the most passive of Messiaen's bird pieces is justified, if not intrinsically, at least in the light of his development. In *Oiseaux Exotiques* for piano and wind instruments (1955) he had already indicated how the recording of natural phenomena might be used to creative and visionary ends. Despite its debt to the birds, this music makes a new sound which, if it reminds us of any other music, suggests affinities with some of the polyrhythmic work of Ives. This fact alone would seem to indicate that Messiaen's abnegation of the will is not necessarily a denial of his humanity; and it prepared the way for the great *Chronochromie* of 1960, a work for large orchestra which is one of those rare pieces that make history. It would seem to complete Messiaen's "magical" retreat from humanism, for the structure is based not on human awareness of progression in time, but on rhythmic proportions inherent in Nature, at once preordained and permutatory, like crystal formation and snow flakes. In a music wherein "Nature is the supreme resource—an inexhaustible treasure-house of sounds, colors, forms and rhythms, and the unequaled model for total development and perpetual variation" (as Messiaen has put it), the ticking of the clock is no longer relevant, and the melodic material, derived from the imitation of specific (and specified) birds, has no more need of thematic growth than have the bird carolers themselves. The astonishing dawn chorus for a plethora of solo strings becomes a climax only in the sense that it attains the maximum of heterophonic freedom. Hermes was a winged messenger, Papageno a feathered child of Nature, and Messiaen's birds are angelic presences who can be free of humanly imposed restraints—such as tonality, "accepted" musical timbre, and so on. They are a manifestation of the flux and perhaps of the female principle, as are the waterfall images which also appear in this work.

The return to Nature "in and for herself," as a release from human complexity, has a long heritage in the music of our time. Perhaps it begins with the bird that sings to Siegfried from the dark forest; certainly it is evident in Debussy's *Nuages* and in the marvelous night pieces of Bartók, with their onomatopoeic representations of chittering birds and barking frogs. In all these, however, Nature's otherness is seen, or rather heard, in opposition to the human: the broken cor anglais phrase that wanders through Debussy's clouds suggests man's littleness against the vast sky, while the middle section of the slow movement of Bartók's *Music for strings, celesta and percussion* juxtaposes man's melodic-harmonic endeavor against the timeless continuum of the (preconscious) sounds of the natural world. Apart from the Parisian-American Edgard Varèse (whom we shall discuss later), Messiaen is the first composer who seeks to reassert man's validity not in conflict with, but as part of, the principles—if not the "laws"—of Nature. He, more than any other single composer of our time, represents modern man's weariness with a literate, will-dominated, patriarchal culture, and his desire to rediscover a matriarchal culture that worships the White Goddess and accepts the Terrible Mothers. It is not an accident that Messiaen's formal sequence of "Anacrusis," "Accent" and "Desinence" parallels the lunar calendar, nor that the processes of rhythmic and intervallic metamorphosis which he began to explore in the *Etudes de modes rhythmiques* of 1949 have direct affinities with the transmutation techniques of the old alchemists, both medieval and Arabian. Indeed, the fact that alchemy has again become a respectable subject is part of our age's rediscovery of the irrational, our consciousness of the unconscious. In a profound sense Messiaen is a musical alchemist, for he is concerned with the nature of Matter (in this case sound-matter) in itself; with the possibility of *changing* matter not through man's will, but by way of an understanding of its laws; and with the ultimate possibility of man himself being reborn through achieving identity with the multiplicity of matter, so that the All becomes the One. A re-cognition of magic and of the chthonic forces that surround us may, of course, release only evil, as it did in Hitler's Germany. But it may also release unsuspected positive powers, in so far as an understanding of natural process may become identical with a fulfillment of the self. In a very real sense Messiaen, in his music, loses the self in order that he may find it, which must be why the man who suffers and rejoices is instantly recognizable in the idiom of the mind that creates. It is pertinent to note that the strophic and antistrophic structure of *Chronochromie* is analogous to the chorus of an ancient Greek tragedy. Certainly, having listened to the piece, we feel that the springs of our humanity have been not relinquished but renewed. Without denying his Christian heritage, Messiaen has attempted to heal the breach that Christianity has committed us to, by reasserting the spiritual validity of the sexual impulse, and rediscovering the identity of the Creator with Created Nature.

So far we have traced the two strands that, becoming intertwined, gave impetus to the "New Music." Webern, harking back to Schoenberg, dissolves beat and pulse, and disintegrates harmony into line, recreating a serialism that has affiliations with the Law of the Gothic motet (which was the twilight of the Middle Ages), and reaching out intuitively toward conceptions more typical of oriental than of occidental cultures. Debussy, the complementary figure, dissolves his Wagnerian harmonic sensuality into quasi-Eastern arabesque; his successor Messiaen seeks to heal the breach between Creator and Created by a fusion of Christian with Buddhist and, indeed, pagan pantheism. If Schoenberg inverted European history (in so far as in *Moses* the Idea is inexpressible, and cannot become manifest in created nature), Webern and Messiaen between them look toward a new—and also a very old—conception of music as Revelation rather than as Incarnation. Today Pierre Boulez, now the Old Master of the avant-garde, consciously rejects those elements in their work which relate to the immediate past. *Schoenberg est mort;* but Webern isn't, any more than is Messiaen or Debussy. The new-old, pre-Renaissance, non-Western elements in Debussy, Webern and Messiaen are his initial impulse. These are reinforced by certain neoprimitive rhythmic conceptions from Stravinsky (especially *The Rite of Spring*), and by certain melodic and textural elements suggested by Schoenberg's *Pierrot Lunaire,* which Boulez admits to be one of the seminal masterpieces of our time.

Of recent years Boulez has deservedly won fame as a conductor; his performances of the music referred to in the previous paragraph are profoundly revealing in reference to his own composition. For instance, his playing of the Webern *Symphony* is, strictly speaking, a revelation; what it reveals is the continuity of lyrical line beneath the apparent fragmentation. The song sings in a metaphysical heaven, infinitely far off; yet, supported by a structure of fine steel, sing it does, infinitely tender. That it sings, that its structure is aurally intelligible, this is the work's greatness, and it makes most of the music that has been influenced by it seem banal. Complementarily, when Boulez plays Debussy's *Images* his precision of rhythm and meticulous delineation of texture enhance, rather than restrict, spontaneity; he "swings" the music and, as in the best jazz, swing metamophoses harmonic corporeality into spiritual grace. Even in performing *La Mer* Boulez plays down the heroic, "symphonic" element and hands back the music's passionate vagaries to the wind and waves. The dominant ego is at a discount, as it is in his performance of Messiaen's *Oiseaux Exotiques;* the precision of the stresses within the complex texture makes the music sound as though it were *playing itself,* relinquishing the will, like *Nuages,* yet richer and stronger because there is so much more to be relinquished. Having once heard *La Mer* this way, which is surely Debussy's, we never want to hear it again with the customary rhetorical gestures.

Most revealing of all, however, is Boulez's performance of Debussy's last orchestral score, *Jeux,* where the physical energy and painful nostalgia that are still latent beneath the surface of Debussy's marine and Iberian evocations finally evaporate. The ballet concerns a tennis party, and tennis, as we recall from Shakespeare, is a sexy game. But it takes place at twilight and is love play without conclusion. Opening with tritonal whole-tone oscillations that are Tristan's imperfect fourths freed from even the yearning for resolution, the score becomes a flickering within the subconscious. Little, broken, Tristanesque sighs wail on the strings, only to dissipate into coruscating figurations of threes against fours against fives. Mood, tonality and tempo are in flux, by the acceptance of which we are released from memory and desire. So this somber comedy is a musical anticipation of the Theater of the Absurd, just as *Pelléas* had been the first existential opera. No single work is closer to the heart of Boulez's own music, as is immediately evident in the volatile fancy of one of his earliest works, the *Sonatine* for flute and piano.

How this Debussyan heritage merges into that of Webern is revealed in another early work of Boulez, the cantata *Le Soleil des Eaux,* composed in his twenty-second year. The second of the two movements, in which René Char's poem speaks directly of man's betrayal of Nature, tells us that man's hanky-panky with the natural world will result only in his physical annihilation unless he finds self-annihilation in submission to the will of God. The technique is Webernian, but more violent; the savage rhythmic and harmonic contrarieties seek a law beyond the self, a serial principle analogous to the cantus firmus technique of late Gothic music and to the Indian raga and tala. The first movement, however, is more positive, less harried by the Law, more Debussyan in technique. The poem celebrates a lizard's will-less passivity on a rock; he's at once above and beyond, yet envious of, a goldfinch, aggressively involved in love and life and the war between man and nature. Here the disintegration of harmonic tension into points of sonority releases lyricism. The long passages of unaccompanied monody acquire, despite their nervosity, something of the levitating ecstasy of oriental cantillation; even the wide leaps and the fragmentation become air-borne, so that the denial of civilization is a positive act. It is already evident that the spirituality of Boulez's music springs from a sublimation, not a denial, of the body's joy.

In *Le Soleil des Eaux* the two movements still exemplify the unresolved tension between the Webernian and the Debussyan (and Messiaenic) heritage. A complete fusion of the two concepts is effected in Boulez's first mature work, *Le Marteau sans maître*. This work, too, has a surrealistic text by René Char, releasing the mind from consciousness, yet asking too what happens when control of the "hammer" is voluntarily abandoned. What makes *Le Marteau* a historically important work is the manner in which Boulez uncompromisingly faces up to the latent implications of Debussy's and Webern's music: implications which may at first seem to be technical, but which cannot be merely that. Thus, if *Le Marteau* is immediately recognizable as a "new noise" (which occurs infrequently in musical history), it is because the texture is even airier, more floating, more disembodied than that of Webern. The instruments—alto flute, viola, vibraphone and guitar, with a large battery of exotic percussion—are all light in timbre and air-borne, as is the sonority of the Gothic motet. Added to this, the rhythmic disintegration is far more extreme even than in Webern. The implied triplet figurations of Webern become in Boulez fives, sevens, nines and what-else, and these irregular units often have to be played in the time of some other unit, so that each player is working to a different silent pulse which he must feel as best he may. The result of this airy fragmentation, so far as the listener is concerned, is that he becomes hardly aware of pulse or of harmonic density. The terms consonance and dissonance have ceased to have much relevance; what one is aware of is the interplay of timbres and sonorities, in which the actual pitch (and therefore "tonality") is less important than its quality and character—high, low, piercing, soft, long, short, etc. This is the more so because of the fantastically rapid speed of the music. Boulez's typical fast movement goes at about 208 to the minute, whereas Webern's average fast speed is about 160–170. Paradoxically, this makes the feeling of Boulez's music slower, not faster, for the less ability the ear has to distinguish alternations of tension, the more static will be the total effect. This is manifest in Messiaen's bird pieces also, and of course the effect is intentional; in becoming stratospheric, we no longer desire conscious direction.

The serial processes in Boulez, as Robert Craft has shown, are related to this increase in the speed of the figuration, and they further decrease the sense of temporal progression. Webern's fragmentation had meant that the interval rather than the note sequence became the unity and the silences between the intervals could be a part of the latent theme. In Boulez the four forms of the serially ordered twelve semitones are always interval rather than note transpositions. One remembers the intervals but not the relationship of the pitches; that everything is now serialized—dynamics, frequency, articulations and timbre—tends further to reduce the supremacy of pitch. The fact that everything moves in serial sequence means that everything is constantly varied; yet the change is a kaleidoscope, the eternal circle of Buddhist philosophy, for if all is change, change itself is meaningless. The effect of this music, as distinct from the analysis of its technical process, is to create an awareness of the *flux* of reality, in which is included "nature" and the nerves, while at the same time releasing us from the flux into "space" and eternity. Thus its oriental affiliations, like those of Debussy, Webern and Messiaen, are as much philosophical as musical. Because of, rather than in spite of, its complexity and restlessness, the music, if adequately performed, should induce—in Charles Ives's wonderful phrase—"a kind of furious calm." Even more than Webern's music, it is antidramatic, rendering the horrors of the text irrelevant. The preordained conditions within which the ecstatic shimmer of sound occurs create magic, in some ways similar to that created by a Balinese gamelan orchestra, which has a comparable sonority and equally rapid figuration within an almost immobile basic pulse. Though we may not know—as we presumably do, if we are born within the culture, when listening to Balinese music—precisely what the magic signifies, we are nonetheless aware that it has the faculty of release.

Despite this "flux-like" character, *Le Marteau sans Maître* is constructed on a cyclical (not progressive) form that owes much to Messiaen's rondo structures. The first vocal movement is preceded by two instrumental movements: an air-borne chitter of sound scored for flute, vibraphone, guitar and viola, in four sections with strongly marked fermata; and the first commentary on the "Bourreaux de Solitude," which is in effect a flute solo accompanied by percussion, every note being serially organized in dynamics as well as pitch and rhythm. The wide-flung flute line achieves a disembodied ecstasy which is both reinforced and controlled by the fantastically complex tala of the percussion instruments. A wildly disintegrative middle section or trio is scored for xylorimba, pizzicato viola and two bongos, and is followed by a return to the flute's song in telescoped form. The first vocal number, "L'Artisanat Furieux" is a duo for alto voice and flute, in which the relationship to the flute solo movement from *Pierrot Lunaire* is no less obvious than the oriental affiliations of the melismatic style. Despite the enormous leaps and "difficult" intervals, the rhythms float delicately, almost tenderly. All the nervosity comes from the blood-thirsty words. In the marvelous setting of the phrase, *"je rêve la tête sur la pointe de mon couteau le Perou,"* fear and terror are dissipated in the act of creation, as they are in Schoenberg's Pierrot, who is also the murderer of love.

The second commentary on the "Bourreaux de Solitude" is highly nervous and jittery, with elaborate hoqueting comparable with that in some of Stravinsky's recent music. The horror within the mind emerges, to be assuaged in the fantastic, freely soaring lyricism of the second vocal movement, "Bel Edifice et Pressentiments," in which the voice is intertwined with an equally melismatic flute and viola. In the "Bourreaux de Solitude" movement itself the texture is more open, the tala pattern of the maracas more aurally intelligible; this may be why the music sounds convincing as the pivotal point of the eternal circle. The last three movements effect the return. "Après L'Artisanat Furieux" is an interlude related to the first movement, also in four sections separated by four fermata; the third commentary on "Bourreaux de Solitude" is a second "double" related to the first commentary, but comparatively slow. It leads to the double of "Bel Edifice et Pressentiments," which has a brief introduction recalling (without literal repetition) earlier movements. Various phrases built on the augmented fourth fulfill a refrain-like function, and for the first time there is direct recapitulation, or rather flashbacks thrown up on the flux. The music to the words "je rêve la tête" is identical with that in the third movement, only backward, with the guitar playing the first part of the vocal phrase. "J'écoute marcher" also quotes in modified form the *marcheur* passage from the sixth movement, an effect the more striking because it occurs in a music which habitually avoids both recognizable repetition and architectural symmetry. Such reminiscences of the past occur, however, only because the past has ceased to matter, for this movement completes the final sundering of consciousness and of temporality. The *Pierrot Lunaire*-like creepy noises drift into the refrains of the voice, and this lyrical apotheosis is consummated when the flute returns for the coda, accompanied by gongs and interspersed with long silences. The effect is very similar to Japanese temple music; lines no less agile, nervous and twittery than the calligraphy of Paul Klee (whom Boulez, like Webern, greatly admires) fade into reverberations that become slower and slower, calmer and calmer, until they vanish into silence.

We are left unsure whether what is revealed is indeed God's will or merely an emptiness that is better than agony. One's first reaction is to be wary of Western music that attempts to evade progression so completely. But if *Le Marteau sans Maître* seems a fascinating but abortive experience that overstays its welcome, the reason may be not because it goes too far, but because it doesn't go far enough.

Similarly, if we find the *Second Piano Sonata* baffling—except in so far as the slow coda seems beautiful on the analogy of the madman who hammered his head because it was so nice when he stopped—the reason may be that we can't help listening to it traditionally, looking for and missing affiliations with Viennese chromaticism. Boulez himself is said to have referred to it as his Beethovenian sonata, an opinion we can accept only with the eye, and still more the ear, of faith. When, however, he completely finds himself, in *Pli selon Pli,* his largest work to date, he no longer arouses expectations which he can't fulfill. Perhaps because of this he proves that his apparent evasion of human responsibilities may be no such thing.

Two things are immediately obvious about Boulez's prodigious musicianship as revealed in this work. One is the originality and sensuous precision of his aural imagination, which rivals that of Debussy; the other is the sensitivity of his command of vocal line which, with its melismatic grace notes, is now no less nervously agile, yet still more radiantly lyrical, than that of Webern. Boulez's choice of Mallarmé's poems is itself significant, for Mallarmé's "concentric universe" creates an eternal present in which "all is always now" and there can be no historic past or future. It is true that the fluttery tenderness of Boulez's setting roots us in the experience we have lived through, in so far as, during the early stages, the leaping convolutions imply a harmonic density comparable with that of Webern. Gradually, however, we're levitated skyward by the quasi-oriental arabesques, over a variety of celestial-sounding ostinati, until in the second "Improvisation" any preordained serial control is no longer necessary. Abstract supernatural law gives way to the truth of the subconscious mind. The voice becomes purely monodic, floating rhythmless, in unmeasured notation, without harmonic implication, over shimmering drones and reverberating gongs. Yet at this point, when we're most freed from time and space, the clattering hurly-burly of nature comes back in the wild music that Boulez scores for his gamelan orchestra of xylophones, harps, celesta, vibraphone, piano and multitudinous bells, gradually reinforced by normal orchestral instruments playing in quasi-improvisatory heterophony. There's something reminiscent of Varèse's use of the sonorities of the natural world in this movement, as there is in Messiaen's comparable hubbub in *Oiseaux Exotiques.* But whereas Varèse and Messiaen positively evoke the animate world, we experience Boulez's cacophony of nature as an opposite pole to the hermetic calm induced by the vocal monody. Though there's nothing personal, ego-dominated, about the racket (which Boulez conducts chronometrically, as he does the still passages), the effect is to carry us back to the exacerbated bark from which the work had started.

So whereas Beethoven grows through each work progressively more involved in tonal and motivic conflict, seeking ultimate resolution, Boulez begins at a high point of harmonic and rhythmic contrariety, which dissolves in increasingly monodic, nonmetrical, nonharmonic cantillation. He abnegates reason and consciousness to enter nirvana; then the cycle starts again. The title of *Pli selon Pli* presumably refers to the experiential as well as the technical process. So the music isn't a withdrawal into a Japanese temple in order to evade our perplexities; rather, it's a contemporary disassociation from our perplexities in order that we may understand what they are. This may be why Boulez's apparently eccentric work seems so relevant to us, and its hour and a half duration not a moment too long. It's difficult to know how to estimate "greatness" in works that have no beginning, middle and end. But whatever the future has in store for us, and however equivocal this work's position between East and West, we may hazard a guess that it will establish itself as a crucial masterpiece of our time, as Debussy's *Jeux* and Webern's *Symphony* were of theirs.

Boulez was trained as a mathematician and the preordained serialism of musically abstract works such as the *Structures* for two pianos go about as far as humanly operated instruments can hope to go in building musical forms from mathematical proportions—from the laws, such as the vector section, which underlie the cosmos. We can appreciate the logic of this denial of the personal in an increasingly scientific world, and such structures presumably affect our response to the total experience on repeated hearing, even though they cannot be aurally intelligible in an art that exists in time. In a sense one could say that this submission to mathematical process is a culmination of post-Renaissance's man's desire to play God; he becomes the lawgiver, or at least the law-revealer, so that his abnegation of the self is also a final arrogance. Boulez's later career, however, suggests that he's aware of this dubiety of intention. Whether or not the mathematical laws of the cosmos are God's will, it's an inescapable fact that human beings cannot interpret them infallibly, and in the relationship *between* God and man something other than mathematical principle is involved. This is why Boulez has, in part, retreated from "preordained" serialism to some kind of indeterminacy—to a reliance not on mathematical law, nor on the human will, but on the most primitive springs of our nature. There's some evidence to suggest that this is true not merely of *Pli selon Pli* (which employs the human voice even though Mallarmé's words are intentionally devoid of specific "meaning"), but also of his recent, purely instrumental works, which would seem to be organized on mathematico-scientific principles. The *Third Piano Sonata,* still in progress, includes indeterminate elements, and the *Doubles* for orchestra are in three sections which represent a transition from order to flux. The first section, "Figure," is geometrically precise; the second section, "Doubles," effects mutations of the original mathematical proportions, giving at least the illusion of greater freedom; while the last section, "Prism," refracts and splinters the patterns to create a heterophonic hurly-burly strikingly similar to the "cacophony of Nature" in *Pli selon Pli.* It is interesting that this retreat from the Law should be echoed even by the most fanatically doctrinaire of post-Webernian composers, Karlheinz Stockhausen.

He, too, was trained as a mathematical engineer, and found his starting point in a creative misunderstanding of Webern's most difficult and rigidly serial works, opus 14–20. For Stockhausen the "circular" rather than "progressive" implications of Webern's serialism outweigh the expressivity at which Webern still aimed. Works such as the *Kontrapunkte* of 1952 (which are contemporary with Boulez's *Structures* and *Polyphonie X*) go even further than Boulez in total serialization, for "each note is fixed in the time span of the whole musical structure by a conjunction of coordinates which determine its pitch, dynamic, duration and mode of attack." Stockhausen next extended these techniques to what he calls "group forms." In a piece such as *Gruppen* for three orchestras, the individually determined notes are "constellated" into groups (played on the three orchestras), which are in themselves predetermined, but flexible in the relation of one group to another. Thus the individual elements are a microstructure within the macrocosm of the groups. That comparable techniques had been used many years ago by Charles Ives (without the predetermined elements) points to the fact that Stockhausen's release from the "will" implies a simultaneous appeal to mathematics and to the unconscious; the determined and the indeterminate elements will, for him, be complementary.

Zeitmasse for five woodwind, though written for conventional resources, effects a more radical metamorphosis of traditional notions of music than any superficially comparable work of Boulez. "Beat" disappears even more completely, and with it any sense of man's corporeal nature, his heartbeat and physical gestures. Though the title means time measurement, the music concerns time's negation. The serial organization of the rhythms is based on extremely short time values which organize the music into numerical patterns, like the talas of oriental music, only incredibly more rapid and more complicated. Occasionally these patterns may exist over a pulse evident in one part, since if we lost all sense of pulse we wouldn't be aware of what was being relinquished. Against this latent pulse, we feel the loss of beat as exactly parallel to the loss of pitch that occurs when the patterns, in their flickering complexity, shade over from notable pitch to microtonal inflection and to noise. This is strictly comparable with what happens in oriental monody, or in the improvised roulades of a Charlie Parker, Sonny Rollins or John Coltrane, except that they, as jazz musicians, start from a frank admission of a corporeal beat, which the solo line divides into fantastically rapid numerical rhythms, usually involving an Eastern distortion of pitch.

It follows that Stockhausen's music, even more than Boulez's, denies traditional harmonic centrality. Indeed, he abandons tonal notation, using only the sharp sign; and because rather than in spite of the serialization of pitch, rhythm and dynamics seeks an ever greater differentiation between the parts. This is achievable because the parts are less (if at all) concerned about their vertical relationships. In this again Stockhausen resembles Webern in more extreme form, while both may be related to the late Gothic motet, wherein the strangest disparities of text, melody and rhythm were precariously held together by the doctrinal magic of cantus firmus series and of isochronous rhythm. In *Zeitmasse* the ultimate disintegration is just, but only just, suspended. Each instrument has its own preordained time scheme. Sometimes one part may have an implied beat which the others must think against in elaborately numerical rhythms, but the "goal" of the work is the complete disappearance of beat: a condition wherein each part has a distinct metronomic indication as starting point, from which it may accelerate or retard independently of the others. Such unmeasured identity is an ultimate form of the "restlessness" of the Gothic motet. Interestingly, Stockhausen's most typical direction is "as fast as possible," which in aural effect is indistinguishable from his other frequent direction, "as slow as possible," for with the disappearance of pulse goes any sense of movement from or toward. Again, there may be a parallel in the later work of a jazz saxophonist like John Coltrane.

The freeing of music from beat is thus an attempt to escape the limitations of merely human potentiality. This is why this kind of music had to lead to electronic realization, for electronic instruments can perform perfectly rhythms and pitches of which human beings, however skilled, are but dubiously capable. The world of sound is a continuum, as Busoni said many years ago, and the world of our traditional music is but a fraction of a fraction of one diffracted ray from that Sun music which "fills the heavenly Vault with Harmony." This reference to the music of the spheres reminds us how medieval, or non-Western, the implicit philosophy is. Music is becoming Revelation rather than Incarnation again; the substitution of the mathematician's order for the artist's, however, prompts questions which we hardly needed to ask in considering Boulez's *Pli selon Pli.* The medieval composer was at once artist and mathematician; so is the twentieth-century electronic composer. Both are medicine men, promulgating a Mystery. The difference is that although everyone in the Middle Ages knew that God worked in a mysterious way, they had no doubt that his Church was relevant to their everyday lives, whereas the twentieth-century scientist in his laboratory is a mystery man in a somewhat different sense. We regard him with awe, but we can't profess to understand the relevance of his pronouncements to our lives, except in so far as we know that it is within his power to destroy us. This may be why most electronic music doesn't sound like the revelation of a Faith, but rather like creepy space noises for a science-fiction film. And it is a fiction, however scientific; though it fills us with a sense of the unknown, it hardly leaves us feeling that we have conquered space, either without the mind or within it.

Nor have we, of course. We are only beginning to learn what the qualities and potentialities of a new medium are; it is still the com-position, the creation of the musical order, that will give life to the order of engineer and acoustician. It is interesting that although Stockhausen has constructed works according to the most rigid principles of mathematical engineering, he has sometimes (we are told by other scientists) got his mathematics wrong! The Law is illusory; but the value of the composition may lie precisely in the illusion, which is an admission of human fallibility. In Stockhausen's *Kontakte,* for instance, the contacts are between purely electronic sounds, between sounds of metal, wood and skin, and between processed natural noises. The essence of the work is that it is an interplay between mathematical law and the flux of nature; the scale of electronically produced timbres "mediates between" the familiar tones and noises, and "facilitates transformation of sound from each one of these categories into every other one, and mutations of sound into completely new, previously unknown, sound events." While we cannot apply to this music the normal criteria by which we value traditional music, we can see that the criteria we apply to *Zeitmasse* are not irrelevant to it. The patterns may be metrically more complex, the infinite gamut of pitches more widely investigated, the ultimate tempo still more orientally immobile;

nonetheless, human identity still struggles within the spaceship.

That this music is a beginning, however, is important in more than a technical sense. We have referred to the fact that both Webern and Boulez, hypersophisticated artists though they are, were concerned with being "new born," in Paul Klee's sense. Similarly, it is probably not an accident that the piece of electronic music that makes most imaginative sense to us, at least among the works produced in old Europe, should be Stockhausen's *Gesang der Jünglinge,* which is specifically concerned with the theme of childhood and youth. The texture is made up of children's voices, speaking and singing snatches of street songs and nursery tunes; of processed abstractions from vowel sounds and consonants (a human language phonetically transmuted to mathematics); and of pure electronic sounds in which there is no intrusion of the human at all. Thus the piece deals with embryonic human life within the mathematical laws of the cosmos. Human language is literally disintegrated into its component noises—an ultimate form of the process that was manifest, in the twilight of the Middle Ages, in the late Gothic motet. The nonhuman appears to be inimical, destroying the possibility of communication; nonetheless, when apprehensible human words do emerge they prove to be an act of praise, sung by the Man in the Fiery Furnace, from the Book of Daniel. The fiery furnace may be hell, and is certainly our postatomic world; yet, though the gibbers and twitters get faster and fiercer while the children's cries (scattered stereophonically on five loudspeakers in different parts of the hall) grow fainter and more forlorn, the voices are not finally obliterated. Indeed, the disintegration of human language into phonetics and its identity with "abstract" mathematics become a way of reaffirming the human and a potential new life. From its awareness of disintegration, the music praises God; its rebirth is a religious act.

At the time he composed *Gesang der Jünglinge* Stockhausen was formally a Roman Catholic. Though he has since renounced the Church, he remains a mystical composer in the sense that he follows Messiaen in wishing "alchemically" to transmute the material of sound. Indeed, in his case the transmutation analogy is literal, for unlike Messiaen he employs electronic techniques to change the quality of sound matter itself. (In *Microphony No. 1,* for instance, two players stroke, tickle and hit an enormous Chinese tam-tam while two other performers transmute the reverberations by the application of contact microphones.) Since alchemy is in part a rediscovery of the irrational which is inherent in Nature, it is not surprising that in all his later works Stockhausen has tended to emphasize the variable and indeterminate elements in his music at the expense of the predetermined elements. Some of the *Klavierstücken,* or the *Refrain* for three performers, employ sound fragments of which the order, and to some extent the character, is determined by the performer. The concept of progression, of beginning, middle and end, which we have seen to be largely irrelevant to Boulez's music, is here entirely meaningless; the form of *Klavierstück X,* for instance, is described by Stockhausen as the *augenblick* —the instantaneous glance of the eye, in which every "event" is coexistent with every other. There is a direct parallel here with primitive visual art, as well as music; the art of the Eskimos, for instance, is a multidirectional and nontemporal filling-up of space which can be seen equally well from any direction, so that our notion of a "right side up" only excites their mirth.

It would seem that most of Stockhausen's later music implies at least a partial return from the duality of the Christian Cross and from Montaigne's depiction of "passage rather than Being" to the circular processes of the East and of primitive cultures. The key work in Stockhausen's later career is specifically entitled *Zyklus.* In the score of this extended work for one percussion player "sixteen pages of notation have been spiral-bound to one another," Stockhausen says, "side by side"; there is no beginning and no end. "The player may start on whichever page he pleases, but he must then play a cycle in the given succession. During the performance the player stands in the center of a circle of percussion instruments and turns, from one playing position to another, once around his own axis, clockwise or counterclockwise, depending on the direction in which he has chosen to read. Areas combining dots and groups of notes and symbols vary from one another through differences in the number of possible combinations; they mediate continuously, in their composed succession, between the entirely unequivocal and the extremely ambiguous. The structure with the greatest indeterminateness, the most ambiguous form, is shaped in such a way that it comes to be almost indistinguishable from the immediately following, most firmly fixed structure. Thus one experiences a temporal circle in which one has the impression of moving constantly in the direction toward ever-increasing ambiguousness (clockwise) or certainty (counterclockwise), although at the critical point at which the extremes touch, the one imperceptibly turns into the other. The purpose is to close the open form through the circle, to realize the static state within the dynamic, the aimless within the aimed, and not to exclude or destroy one aspect or another, not to seek a synthesis in a third state, but rather to attempt to eliminate the dualism and to mediate between the seemingly incompatible, the utterly different."

This may seem a tall order for one percussion player; yet the work is powerful enough, at least as interpreted by the phenomenal Christoph Caskel, to stand as a *locus classicus* of musical-philosophical principle. "To eliminate the dualism" has certainly been the impulse behind all Stockhausen's recent music, and the traditional post-Renaissance dichotomies between sound and noise, content and form, composer and performer, performer and audience are in a state of flux, if not finally broken down. It's no longer a question of the artist in relationship "to" society, for if the artist is the creator, the maker of order, yet as he makes his world, so simultaneously is he made by it. Stockhausen's immense, seventy-five-minute *Momente* is a case in point, summing up his creative career up to this stage (1965), and employing his group forms, collective forms, variable forms and multiple forms in powerfully convincing relationship.

The work is in fact scored for "natural," not electronic, vocal and instrumental resources, but these are of astonishing variety: soprano solo, four choirs and thirteen wind and percussion instruments (including two electronic organs). The piece opens with desultory clapping by the choirs, interspersed with random "Bravo's" and "Pfui's"—expressions of approval and disapproval. As the music unfolds we hear a main text (mostly allocated to the soprano solo) which is biblical, but taken not from the Book of Daniel this time, but from that great paean to eroticism, the Song of Songs. This text (which should be sung in the language native to the audience) and the wide-spun lyricism of the solo line are again an affirmation; they are surrounded by other fragmentary texts in several real languages and one invented (nonsense) language, spoken, yelled and screamed, sometimes disintegrated phonetically into syllables that are "pure sound" (as in *Gesang der Jünglinge*), but sometimes retaining intelligibility. Whatever the nature of the texts, which the composer picked at random from his reading during the period of composition, the point would seem to lie in the crucial aphorism of William Blake: "He who kisses the Joy as it flies/ Lives in Eternity's sunrise." To live in the moment is to obliterate Time and defy contrarieties, and the work consists of "moments" precisely because we are *involved in* an aural universe, in which there is no dramatic sequence, and no division between the objective reality of the external world and our subjective response to it. The relevance of such a conception to the world we're beginning to live in is obvious. Instant speeds are abolishing time and space and, in Marshall McLuhan's words, the "mechanical principle of analysis in series has come to an end"; any number of different acts can be simultaneously synchronized on magnetic tape.

More than any other European composer of our time, Stockhausen is engaged in writing the history of the future because, as Wyndham Lewis put it, he is more aware than most of us of the nature of the present. It's hardly surprising that the immediacy of such awareness should be, in *Momente,* of such lacerating sonorous intensity as to approach hysteria. Yet the hysteria isn't the composer's but is rather what the world—our "human predicament" in the present—does to us; the composer's function may be precisely to *compose* us, to help us to accept, and therefore to sing our love song from, the violence that surrounds us. Moreover, although sounds of the external world—laughter, sighs, whispers, croaks, wails—occur in what appears to be the random sequence one might experience them on the street or in the subway, yet at the same time these sounds and noises are shaped by the mind of the artist. Fortuitous clapping may become a notated rhythmic pattern; the heterophonic and statistically rhythmed first section will be balanced against a largely homophonic middle section, and that against the third section's fusion of heterophony and polyphony in more traditionally notated meters. The recurrent magnificent refrains for chorus and brass remind us that traditional notions of the human imagination and even of will are not entirely discounted in Stockhausen's new, "momentary" universe of sound. This music may be profoundly appropriate to our embryonic society founded on electronic technology. In the strict sense this is a synthetic music for our synthetic culture, for it brings together and alchemically synthesizes as many aspects as possible of experience and of sound matter, embracing elements of non-Western and primitive music, as well as noise which is not strictly notatable.

We shall see later that only in America (in the sequence of Ives, Varèse, John Cage and Earle Brown) can one find a comparably radical development. But if Stockhausen is by far the most forward-looking of European composers, his attempt to eradicate dualism has had an effect even on music which accepts more traditionally humanist premises as a starting point. Luigi Nono, for instance, began from a vivid apprehension of humanism's failure; if human cruelty and injustice, under the shadow of the mushroom cloud, is as it is, then one has to seek a law that isn't humanly arbitrary. So his acceptance of rigid serial principles, in every aspect of composition in his earlier works, was related to his acceptance of Communist dialectic: but for the Law, both music and society might collapse in hysteria. Though *Polifonica-Monodia-Ritmica* of 1951 is on every level among the strictest of serial compositions, it achieves, by way of the tenuity of its texture, a relaxed passivity that sounds (especially in the second and third movements) almost Japanese, with an additive rhythmic series of drums and gongs. However, Nono soon abandoned this unequivocal reliance on an external law in discovering, as Boulez and Stockhausen did contemporaneously, that rebirth can happen only within the psyche. The technical developments of his music, such as his partial relinquishment of pitch and harmony in favor of the *campo sonoro* or sound field, are a manifestation of this spiritual change. Thus, the first three movements of *Il Canto sospeso* are in the post-Webernian, pointilliste manner, serially organized, with elaborate, tala-like rhythmic permutations; the lack of metrical pulse, the *latent* lyricism, the rarefied sonority extend, without radically modifying, Webern's principles. In the fourth movement, however, Nono introduces a semitonic note cluster on strings, long sustained, with individual notes picked out in sequence by wind instruments. Interval and harmony are no longer the point: the cluster is a "density" (in Varèse's sense) covering from two to twelve semitones, interlocking in different dynamics and durations. In *Canciones a Guiomar* the process is extended to quarter-tone clusters, and also to unnotatable pitches, since the instruments are mainly percussive with complex overtone resonances, like Japanese temple gongs. For Nono the orchestra is no longer a polyphonic-harmonic medium. Brass, woodwind and strings are separate consorts, and the percussion group is a separate band with its own dynamic and pitch relationships. Several works are scored for voices with percussion; the tender *Liebeslied* of 1954 is for chorus with harp, vibraphone, bells, timpani and cymbals, while the *Cori di Didone* of 1958 employs chorus in thirty-two parts with eight suspended cymbals and four gongs of different sizes, the tone-clusters revolving around the numbers 9, 7, 5, 3.

The gradual elimination of harmony instruments from Nono's music reflects a spiritual as well as technical change. The instrumental texture is disintegrating into "noise," but the noise is a background to words (usually of urgently contemporary implication). Although these words are syllabically fragmented as they are in Stockhausen or in the Gothic motet, the point is nonetheless that the voice sings them. In *Il Canto sospeso* the human voices echo, against the reverberating percussion, not merely from the Nazi prison camp wherein the letters were written, but from an immense, empty cavern—which becomes a womb, in which life may lyrically begin again. Vocal monody is thus the essence of Nono's music, as it is of Boulez's *Pli selon Pli,* and we can understand why he said that for the contemporary composer the central problem is how to write a melodic line. Nono's music has an Italianate lyrical fluidity, and if the lyricism seems pitifully broken, the isolated notes of what would be a continuous line echoing into emptiness, he nonetheless makes us feel that these fragments are shored against our ruin. Perhaps against his intention, his music has become a religious, even a mystical, act. Rebirth within the psyche is the only point we may grow from, in an atomized world; no political panacea can provide a solution.

Another Italian composer of Nono's generation, Luciano Berio, having less direct affiliation with an authority outside the self (whether it be the Roman Church or the Communist Party), has accepted this *ab ovo*ism more readily, without equivocation. This is evident in an abstract instrumental work, using electronic resources, such as *Différences* (1958–60). The differences in question are between "live," humanly operated instruments (flute, clarinet, harp, viola and cello) and tapes of the same instruments modified by electrical-acoustical techniques. The cello, recorded directly on a central loudspeaker, acts as liaison between the human and the nonhuman. In describing the music as "a modern music in the spirit of the commedia dell'arte," Henri Pousseur neatly indicates the music's combination of improvisatory spontaneity with a near-ironic detachment. The work's "aural illusion" is typical—some might say symptomatic—of our time, in that it discredits "reality." The experience is Absurd, in the theatrical sense; if its exploration of the electronic renewal of material and form is in one sense a renewal of our (not merely musical) consciousness as Berio says it is, in another sense it is a liberation from what Boulez called "robotism."

Certainly it is not an accident that Berio's most justly celebrated work, *Circles,* should directly involve theatrical elements, and should be a setting of poems by E. E. Cummings, the aboriginal

New World poet of the Now and Is, who sought for the springs of life in dreams, in coition and in a preconscious abnegation of the Will. Predetermined elements exist in it insofar as the five movements set three poems in a circular ABCBA structure. But this is the "existential" dimension of the piece; it is a serpent eating its own tail because it's an "Is" without precedence or consequence. This allows scope for the unconsciousness of improvisation and favors indeterminacy of pitch from both the singing-speaking-yelling voice and from the mainly percussive instrumental ensemble. Thus, like Varèse's early *Offrandes,* the work is a logical extension of Debussyan impressionism, rather than of Webernian serialism (a relationship still more obvious in the lovely, radiantly airy settings of poems from Joyce's *Chamber Music,* which date from 1953). Certainly Berio has found, for *Circles,* his ideal text, for Cummings's poems are the sensory moment as an end in itself. Sing-speak the poems as Cummings's typography indicates and they become music in which "any relevant action is theatrical." If you're as marvelously natural a musician as Berio, and as superbly vital a singing actress as Cathy Berberian, the work is as good as made for you. Essentially a music of beginnings, *Circles* is a blessedly simple, even simple-minded, piece. The miraculous conclusion—or rather inconclusion, for the voice floats as though reborn from the murmuring mists and the "chime and symphony of Nature"—does what had to be done. We should be grateful for it, even though man, having gone through so much, can hardly be forever content to live childishly in an eternal present, and even though Berio himself may never take the next step that will reawaken consciousness and the tragic sense.

Like *Momente* and much of Stockhausen's recent music, Berio's *Circles* creates and involves one in a world; in its way it, too, is a piece of musical "theater," and we may note also that Nono has given a ritualistic or dramatic projection to most of his recent works. Again, the barriers are broken, and among the barriers shattered is that between the Old World and the New. Both Stockhausen and Berio spend much of their time in the United States, and *Circles,*

VI

The New Music in a New World: Parallel Lines in Jazz and Pop

It has been difficult for European composers, with so much past behind them, to release themselves from "the pain of consciousness." But we have in this book traced how it gradually happened, in considering how Schoenberg is Wagner's successor, and Webern, Schoenberg's, how Messiaen follows Debussy, and how Webern and Messiaen effect the transition to Boulez and Berio. In all of them there is a partial retreat from the West, and an affiliation with techniques and philosophies having contact with pre-Renaissance Europe and, still more, with oriental cultures. But the transition has been hard, and is still uneasy, whereas the American retreat from the West has been more empirically spontaneous. This is natural enough, both because America has less consciousness of the past, and also because her polyglot culture, Janus-like, faces East as well as West. Even in the central figures of the American scene one finds elements that are in part a denial of the West: consider the final movements of Ives's *Concord Sonata* and of the *Piano Sonata* of Copland, both the creation of great American humanists. So it isn't surprising that avant-garde tendencies should have been manifest in American music as far back as the years of the First World War, nor that they should have more to do with Debussyan empiricism than with Webernian serialism. One of the key works in the early history of "progressive" music in America is the extraordinary *Piano Sonata* that Charles Griffes wrote in 1917, the last year of his short life. This employs static Debussyan harmonies and Scriabinesque "raga" formations to generate, from Eastern techniques, a peculiarly Western frenzy. Sophisticated though the idiom is, this music of the asphalt jungle could have been created only in America. Still more typical is a phenomenon like Henry Cowell, who is what Debussy might have been, shorn of most of his genius, and brought up in the streets of San Francisco and on farms in the Midwest, by parents who believed that children, like plants, should be left to grow.

Cowell was familiar with Chinese theater music, Japanese children's street songs and American fiddle music before he knew anything about Brahms or Beethoven. He played the fiddle by ear at the age of five, and began his composing career at the age of eight, not so far behind Mozart. He composed empirically, experimenting with the noises he could extract from an upright piano. Debussy's moment of sensation becomes, with him, the (American) Moment of Sensation, with a capital M and S. But although the composition in the piano pieces Cowell produced during his teens is rudimentary, their sound sensation remains invigorating after forty-odd years. In a piece called *The Banshee,* a piano's strings become a harp capable of an infinite gamut of pitches; the experiment has become the experience. This is the work of an aboriginal, the American Boy in the Woods, who didn't lose his innocence when, grown up, he acquired some academic know-how. Cowell's vastly prolific later output is not very good music, and he's a figure of historical rather than of intrinsic interest. Nonetheless, we can see from his youthful piano pieces why he has become a father figure to the American avant-garde, and it's this quality of ab-originality that sometimes makes American avant-garde music more congenial than its European counterpart.

Certainly the quality is present in the major figure of the older generation, Edgard Varèse, who was (significantly) born in Paris, and became an American citizen in 1916. He called the first work to which he owns *Amérique,* because it was a New World of sound. But if one listens to his *Offrandes,* written in 1921, one can hear how this new world—like that of his friend, colleague and contemporary, Charles Griffes—is related to the world of Debussy. Varèse has told us that, as a young man, he admired Debussy above all composers "for his economy of means and clarity, and the intensity he achieved through them, balancing with almost mathematical equilibrium timbres against rhythms and textures, like a fantastic chemist." The chemical metaphor is significant, and links up with Varèse's complementary admiration for Satie, who wrote "some rather remarkable music, such as the Kyrie from his *Messe des Pauvres,* a music which always reminds me of Dante's *Inferno,* and strikes me as a kind of pre-electronic music." Varèse thus saw Debussy and Satie as a starting point for his own experiments, since if one liberates the chord from antecedence and consequence, the logical step is to proceed to the liberation of the individual sound. This is not just a technical procedure; it is also a new (and at the same time very old) musical philosophy. Varèse must be the earliest composer to reject the Renaissance conception of art as expression and communication; music he composed during the twenties anticipates by thirty years some of the discoveries of the mid-twentieth-century avant-garde. Bypassing twelve-note serialism (which he regards as a musical "hardening of the arteries" because of its dedication to notated, equal-tempered pitch), he makes manifest the prophecies of Busoni in his *Entwurf einer Neuen Aesthetick der Tonkunst:* he is at once a magical composer like Messiaen and a scientific composer like Stockhausen, demonstrating that the two types are in fact complementary in that they effect a revelation, rather than an incarnation, of natural law. Dedekind said of mathematicians: "We are a divine race, and possess the power to create." To live in a scientific-mathematical universe is inevitably to lose consciousness of self; and it is significant that Varèse, who had some scientific training and as a youth considered the possibility of becoming a mathematical engineer, should, in naming one of his works *Arcana,* specifically relate the revelation of natural order to the activities of the alchemists.

So it is not surprising that Varèse's highly sophisticated music should be also primitive (and often oriental), in the sense that it does not involve harmony, but rather consists of nondeveloping patterns and clusters of noises of varying timbre and tension. These interact in a manner that Varèse has compared, in detailed if inaccurate analogy, to rock-formation and crystal mutation:

I was not influenced by composers as much as by natural objects and physical phenomena. As a child, I was tremendously impressed by the qualities and character of the granite I found in Burgundy. . . . And I used to watch the old stone-cutters, marvelling at the precision with which they worked. They didn't use cement, and every stone had to fit and balance with every other. . . .

This conception of music as sound-architecture survives when the development of electronic resources finally gave Varèse an opportunity to "realize" his theories. Whether through indirect human agency or electronics, composition for Varèse is "process":

I am fascinated by the fact that through electronic means one can generate a sound instantaneously . . . you aren't programming something musical, something to be done, but using it directly, which gives an entirely different dimension to musical space and projection. For instance in the use of an oscillator, it is not a question of working against it or taming it, but using it directly without, of course, letting it use you. The same pertains to mixing and filtering. To me, working with electronics is composing with living sounds, paradoxical though that may appear.*

Nothing could be further from the mathematically determined electronic music of composers such as Milton Babbitt. Of Babbitt, Varèse has said:

He wants to exercise maximum control over certain materials, as if he were *above* them. But I want to be *in* the material, part of the acoustical vibration, so to speak. Babbitt composes his materials first and then gives it to the synthesizer, while I want to generate something directly by electronic means. In other words, I think of musical space as open rather than bounded, which is why I speak of projection in the sense that I want simply to project a sound, a musical thought, to initiate it, and then let it take its own course.

Nonetheless, Varèse's music does not take the ultimate step to

* From an interview reprinted in *Composer.*

completely open forms and improvisation. In one sense his music is more closely rooted in traditional concepts than is the recent music of Messiaen and Boulez, let alone Stockhausen, for it still implies some kind of dichotomy between Nature and the Self. The structure of a comparatively recent work such as *Deserts* (1953) may seem to be independent of the will's volition, but the controlling force is still the human imagination. It achieves a powerful image of man's isolation, while enabling him to come to terms with the alien universe in which he exists. The music explores the deserts of wind, of sand and sea and rock, of the city street and of those vaster deserts within the human mind. Normal orchestral wind instruments interact with electronically processed natural sounds (of wind, sea, street and factory), while a large percussion band serves as liaison between the human and the nonhuman world. The humanly operated "noise" of the percussion doesn't seem to save the human from being threatened by the nonhuman in a series of cumulatively increasing tensions, and the end of the work, in which the noise fades into the eternal silence, is grim rather than assuaging. Nonetheless, there is grandeur, as well as excitement, in Varèse's attempt to emulate, through human means, the processes of Nature. If the music is frightening, because it admits that the human ego has lost touch with natural order, it is also unafraid, because the admission helps us to live again.

Maybe only God can make a tree, but Man at least can make sounds behave like crystals; in this sense, there is a powerful affirmation behind Varèse's bringing together of the aural disparities of the natural world. Whereas Ives, who in some of his music attempted something comparable, was content to be humanly amorphous, Varèse sought the scientist's precision, which could not ultimately be achieved because an artist, being human, is humanly fallible. In this respect, Varèse has more in common with a visual artist like Jackson Pollack than with Ives, or with any earlier musician; both Varèse and Pollack seek to *reveal* the (basically mathematical?) order inherent in the natural world. This is the artist's new social justification, if justification is necessary, as Harry Partch, another senior "progressive," seems to think it is. Like

Cowell, and unlike Varèse, whose background is both sophisticated and European, Partch is an American aboriginal, brought up in the parched and parching wastes of Arizona and New Mexico. From his earliest years he rejected the paraphernalia of harmonized music, rediscovered the justly intoned monody and the rhythms of primitive and oriental cultures, and designed his own instruments, which are tuned to a forty-three-tone-to-the-octave scale, and are capable of fairly extensive monophonic, if not harmonic, tonal organization. But this turn to the East is as instinctive, as nonwillful, as that of Varèse. We may see this if we compare Varèse's *Deserts* with Partch's *Windsong,* which was written as an accompaniment to a cinematic version of the Apollo and Daphne story, and which deals specifically with the metamorphosis, indeed the loss, of human identity in the contemplation of the immense solitudes of (American) Nature, of the nonhuman world. Varèse's score sometimes reminds us of the distonated screech of Japanese gagaku music, while Partch's score reminds us of the infinitely slow, microtonal wail of Japanese koto music; yet in both cases the affinity comes not from imitation, but from the attempt to create musical images for emptiness, space and nontemporality.

Normally, however, Partch is a magic composer who, like Carl Orff in Europe, relates music directly to theatrical action; both want to renew a moribund society by rediscovering the instinctual springs of life. Partch thinks the proper function of music is that which it fulfilled in classical Greek drama. His own "musicals" may be considered as an American version of the still vital popular tradition of the Japanese kabuki theater, aiming at a renewal of modern life by incantation, by "spiritual" monody and by "corporeal" rhythm. In *The Bewitched,* described as a "Dance-Satyr," four lost Musicians consult an aged Seer, seeking a remedy for the ills of the modern world, and learn that they already possess, in being true to the moment, the only truth that is humanly apprehensible: "Truth is a sandflea; another moment must find its own flea." So the Musicians are also Clowns, divine fools, and outsiders, bums, hobos—like Partch himself, who for eight years lived by riding the rails. When social satire and musical parody dissolve into what Partch calls slapstick, the resulting dadaism links contemporary nonvalues to values so old that they seem eternal. Human beings who microtonally yell, moan, shout, wail, guffaw or grunt in jazzy abandon or hysteria may become indistinguishable from hooting owls, barking foxes and the wild cats of the woods. But in returning, below consciousness, to Nature, they may rediscover their true selves. In the prelude to scenes 8 to 10, the wailing pentatonic chant evokes an age-old quietude that is nonetheless full of longing. Significantly, it is based on a cantillation of the Cahuilla Indians—aboriginal Americans who live in the emptiness of the Californian deserts. This weird chant, sounding the more disturbing against the wavering ostinati of Partch's forty-three-tone reed organs, reminds us simultaneously of what home means, and of what it means to be homeless.

In Partch's theater works jazz appears, usually parodistically. But jazz isn't only a negative force; it's also part of our intuitive rediscovery of our passional life. It has had so pervasive an influence because, starting as the outcry of a dispossessed race, it came to stand simultaneously for the protest of man alienated from Nature, and as a reminder of the corporeal vigor that modern man has surrendered. So it isn't surprising that jazz, in America, has undergone a development parallel to that in the music we have discussed. Ornette Coleman is a jazz saxophonist who, during the formative years of his career, couldn't read musical notation, though he has since taken lessons with Gunther Schuller. Thus his "composition" was inevitably spontaneous, like that of primitive oral cultures. In a piece such as *Lonely Woman* there is, of course, a corporeal beat such as is alien to the music of Varèse, if not Partch, but against the implicit beat the drumming is of almost oriental complexity, numerical and additive rather than divisive. Moreover, there is no harmony instrument, and the minimum of harmonic implication. The solo voices, overriding the beat with Charlie Parker–like freedom, collide in dissonant heterophony, and the lines are not only of extreme rhythmic flexibility, they are also fragmented, disrupted by silence. Despite the sophistication, the effect is disturbingly primitive, like a more distraught and nervous version of the field holler, wherein the Negro cried out his isolation to the empty fields.

In his most recent work Ornette Coleman—in part stimulated no doubt by the phenomenally virtuosic and beautiful string bass playing (both bowed and plucked) of David Izenzon—has developed the oriental aspects of his art in a positive direction: in no sense could one use the word primitive about as haunting and magical a performance as their *Dawn*. It is also worth noting that a white jazz clarinetist, Jimmy Giuffre, has—on a somewhat lower level of musical invention—taken the ultimate step in dispensing with "beat" altogether, creating a true improvised monody in complex numerical rhythms, again with effects of pitch distortion (achieved by split reeds and overblowing) that have affinities with Asiatic techniques. These strange nocturnal bird and animal, as well as human, noises link up with Varèse and Partch; with the sound, if not the philosophy, of electronic music; and with both the technique and the philosophy of the music of John Cage.

For Cage's music, no less than the jazz surrealism of the later Ornette Coleman and Jimmy Giuffre, is a descent below consciousness and an abnegation of the Will. The parallel between Partch and Cage's early music is also close, for both discarded harmony and returned to music as incantation, conceived monophonically in line, numerically in rhythm. Cage's "night music," *She Is Asleep* (and maybe dreaming), is scored for wordless voice and prepared piano, and is a ritual murmuring of the unconscious comparable to Partch's aboriginal chants and to Giuffre's solo clarinet. Similarly, Cage's *Sonatas and Interludes* for prepared piano remind us of the Polynesian sounds of Partch's invented instruments, with an occasional hint of disembodied jazz, if the appropriately paradoxical expression be permitted. These pieces are highly musical and very beautiful, but Cage apparently came to think that their "chronometric" construction on ragas and talas was no less an evasion than the chromatic serial principle which he had already abandoned in rejecting European harmony. In any case he gave up humanly preordained structures and handed composition over to chance operations: the toss of a coin, the throw of dice, the noting of accidental imperfections in the manuscript paper. Though these methods produced some exciting noises (for instance, the Carillon pieces which sound like Japanese temple bells tolling a paean not to God, but to nothingness), they are in effect identical with the strict serialists' mathematically preordained order; both seek to free music, as far as possible, from subjectivity (the composer's, performer's and listener's) and from human error.

In later works such as the *Concert* for piano and orchestra Cage completes the composer's abdication. He no longer notates his material, but merely offers hints for improvisation. The succession and duration of the parts are dependent on chance operations, and also on the sub- or semiconscious reactions of the participants. Each performance is inevitably different, and while the texture of sound is comparable with that of Varèse, in that the instruments play microtonally in an infinite gamut of pitches, the chaotic amorphousness tends to be relaxed in effect, as compared with Varèse's impersonal order. Varèse's music seems to be beyond conscious volition, like Nature herself, whereas Cage's music, by this time, in fact *is* so, for the forest or the city street takes over from man.

While we can't help feeling that the loss of Cage's aural sensitivity is regrettable, he would consider our objection in the strict sense impertinent, for he is no longer concerned with "so-called music." Indeed, since each player is instructed to play all, any or none of the notes allotted to him, it is theoretically possible, if improbable, that a performance could result in complete silence: an ultimate condition which Cage has indeed realized in his notorious *Four Minutes Thirty-two Seconds* for piano. Clearly this is an end; it may also be a beginning, in that in possessing so completely blank an innocence Cage can be, like Gertrude Stein and Paul Klee, "as though new born, entirely without impulse, almost in an original state." However self-destructive such an attitude may be from our Western standpoint, it is interesting that there should be something like a post-Cage generation of composers in the United States, some of whom are literally a new race of composers in that they have never received, and have no use for, any training in the harmonic traditions of Europe. Certainly the degree of talent exhibited by this group is in no way dependent on conventional expertise. No orthodox training would be necessary to create Morton Feldman's *Durations,* which is scored for a number of instruments all playing from the same part, so that one couldn't hope for a more complete rejection of dualism. They play mostly single, designated pitches, but although they begin simultaneously they are free to choose their own occurrences within a given general tempo. Thus the instruments, in changing combinations, are "reverberations" from a single sound source. The tones are always isolated, immensely slow and delicately soft. Such simultaneous sounds as occur through overlapping of the durations are mostly unisonal or concordant. An infinitely slow drone on muted tuba, a third on muted string harmonics, sound as though the players are creating the tones out of the eternal silence, and we are being born afresh in learning to listen to them. Music seems to have reached the point of extinction; yet the little that is left certainly presents the American obsession with emptiness completely absolved from fear. The rarefied tenderness seems to have the property of making us saner, rather than more mad.

The element of renewal in Feldman's music lies in the fact that choice is once more very important; his isolated sounds are as scrupulously selected as are the isolated chords of Debussy, the composer with whom Feldman has most in common. A more widely relevant type of renewal may be exemplified in the graph pieces and "Available Forms" of another post-Cage composer, Earle Brown, who claims to have learned more from the painting of Pollock and the mobiles of Calder than from any musician, including Cage. His graph pieces (of which the most extreme is *December 1952* for any number and any kind of instruments) notate only high, middle and low registers and densities, and exist only in their mobility, while they are being made. They are not composition, but a stimulus to musical activity; they differ from Cage's later work in that they call for creative instinct on the part of the performers. Brown's later "open form" works precisely notate pitch, timbre and often rhythm, but leave to the performers or conductor the decision as to the order in which the sound events take place. Brown prefers to write for very large resources (his

Available Forms II is scored for ninety-eight instruments with two conductors who preserve independence during performance, though they have carefully rehearsed the sound events); thus, the sound of his music is remote from the hermetic tranquillity of Feldman, and is more comparable with the multiple-group pieces of Ives and Varèse than with the music of Cage. The human agency of the composer (who devised the complex sound events), of the conductors (who decide when and in what order the events shall occur), and of the players (who must play the notes as written, but not necessarily in temporal conjunction with one another) is immensely important. This is true even though Brown prefers to emulate the ambiguities, the "open ends" of Nature, rather than to impose his order on his material, which ranges from noise and "inarticulate sounds" to sounds produced by highly sophisticated musical techniques.

In reinvolving the performer in creation Brown is turning toward action, and in this resembles the composers who seem to have deliberately abdicated human responsibility. At the furthest swing of the pendulum from Europe's post-Renaissance obsession with the will, Cage and his disciples would free us from past and future, inviting us to enter an autonomous Now. Similarly, Robert Rauschenberg at one time painted completely white or completely black canvases, invoking the space, the nothingness within which we may perceive afresh the astonishingly disparate objects (introduced bodily into his later work) of the visible world. For Cage learning-to-hear, for Rauschenberg learning-to-see, are separate from action but not independent of it, since life must be lived in time. This is why "any relevant action is now theatrical," a belief which has been actualized when Cage and Rauschenberg have collaborated with the dancer Merce Cunningham to complement their aural and visual images with movement in time and space.

This movement, however, like the hearing and seeing, has no before and after. There is no expressionist purpose, only a "purposeful purposelessness," in the relationship between movement, sound and image in the work of the Merce Cunningham Dance Group. Thus, in *Suite for Five* the actions—now gay, now anguished, now grotesque—are as diverse as Nature herself; yet in being purged of causation they are purged too of the nag of memory and the tug of desire. This they achieve *through* their lack of relationship to Cage's music, which is even more devoid of progression or motor rhythm than is Japanese temple music. The softly reverberative sounds of the prepared piano, occurring at chronometric points dictated by chance operations, and separated by immense silences, really do cause one to listen anew, while Rauschenberg's almost blank costumes and decor help one to see the actions with unblinkered eyes.

This abstraction is preserved even when the work, such as the ballet *Crises,* seems to involve dramatic implications. Indeed, in this ballet the crises of the title are erotic; yet the actions between the man and four women evade climax. The music is Conlon Nancarrow's celebrated studies for three player pianos. The fantastic complexity of the polyrhythms, which machines can negotiate but which human beings couldn't, transmutes the sexy and nostalgic flavor of jazz and pop into loony hysteria. Yet the sounds preserve, through the mechanization, a disembodied detachment, which communicates itself to the actions. For all the violence of the gestures and the sleaziness of the atmosphere, we are released from our more inchoate appetites in simply accepting them. Even they can take their place with "the permanent emotions of Indian tradition." Merce Cunningham's *Solo* to Christian Wolff's pianistic explosions goes still further, for it induces a therapeutic calm from the neurotic twitch and spastic shiver that we've come to recognize, at least since *West Side Story,* as gestures typical of our world and time. Both the abstraction of the mechanical and the dadaistic release into an eternal Now recall Satie's *Parade;* small wonder that John Cage, himself a Beckett clown, regards Satie with admiration.

The ultimate, rediscovered primitivism of a Cage or a Feldman has parallels, we have seen, in the surrealistic trend in modern jazz. Most interestingly, it is also paralleled by mid-century developments in pop music. Thirty, or even twenty, years ago pop music was still commercial jazz, tied to the Sousa-Foster tradition of hedonism or escape. Today pop music seems, no less than "straight" music, to be affecting another kind of return *ab ovo,* to rhythm and to the most rudimentary line as incantation. The music of Cage or Feldman on the one hand, the Beatles and Bob Dylan on the other, may seem poles apart; nonetheless they have in common a distrust of the personal, of "individual" expression, and both attempt to return to magic, possibly as a substitute for belief. To neither does the Christian ethic, which implies guilt and conscience and the duality of harmony, seem relevant. In the music of Cage there is virtually no corporeal rhythm left; the Mersey beat has nothing much except corporeal rhythm. Yet both, by their complementary if opposite paths, effect a dissolution of Time and of consciousness.* In a very literal sense the rows of nubile young females who faint away at a Beatle performance have found the nirvana that Tristan was seeking, and the ecstasy of being "sent" becomes a communal and collective activity which is also a sundering of identity. The fact that young people dance *alone,* not with partners, to beat music is interesting in itself. They evade the togetherness of relationship with another person (a love relationship, however joyful, will also inevitably hurt) in order to enter into a collective unconsciousness. There's no coming together of individuals; their lonesomeness merges into a corporate act, and belonging to the group asserts one's livingness, such as it is. In this way the ritual value of the sound is inseparable from its musical nature. Its melodic and harmonic material is rudimentary, its rhythmic appeal obvious in its excess (contrary to popular opinion beat music never swings, only beats, for jazz-swing implies a subtle tension between metrical accent and melodic phrasing). The essential characteristics of beat music are that its phrases are very brief and are hypnotically re-

* "It is perhaps the essential character of consciousness that it is not just a picture of what is happening at one instant of time or an infinitely thin cross-section of process. Consciousness introduces the time-dimension as a reality, linking the no-longer-existing past with the actual present in what is called perception or recognition, and forecasting a merely possible future on lines influenced by wish and purpose. Process and purpose are thus inseparable in our minds from the beginning. . . . It is significant in this connection that the repressed unconscious mind is said to be 'timeless,' suggesting that the loss of 'span' is one of the factors in repression." (Ian Suttie: *The Origins of Love and Hate*)

peated; that its rhythm is obvious and unremitting; and that its sonority is very loud. Through its rudimentariness, its unremittingness, and its loudness it provides a substitute for security, or a pretence that we, the young, in an insecure world, can stand—or dance—on our own feet.

One may doubt whether it is pervasively erotic, for the eroticism of jazz depends precisely on the swinging equilibrium between line and rhythm which beat music lacks. In this connection it is interesting that the musical origins of beat music were not in traditional jazz or even in the commercialized forms of jazz which were the pop music of the thirties and forties; rather, they were in the most primitive and rudimentary form of the country blues, which had begun not as a music of social (let alone sexual) intercourse, but as the solitary "holler" in the empty fields. Created by a deprived, dispossessed, alienated, persecuted minority, the country blues became the impetus to the mass-music of young people in a mass-civilization. We can trace the process whereby this happened by listening to some specific examples. Howlin' Wolf, yelling a field holler, attempts to "send" himself beyond personal distress by the monodic, incantatory repetition of a three-note wail, basically pentatonic, using techniques of pitch distortion and rhythmic ellipsis that have the remotest and most primitive ancestry. This folk tradition still survives in the urban blues, as we can hear in *Fare Well Blues* as performed by a white singer, Barbara Dane. The effect of this most moving performance depends largely on the fact that the "primitive" elements in vocal inflection and rhythmic displacement are at odds with the hymnbook-derived harmony of the blues guitar; the age-old monodic melancholy of the voice seems the more searing against the harmonic prison of "civilization." As folk art merges into pop, the prison, at least at a superficial level, has to be accepted. Two stages in this process can be observed in different versions of *Alabama Bound*. Leadbelly and Woodie Guthrie still employ primitive folk techniques of vocal production and rhythmic distortion, while at the same time subduing these wilder qualities to a regular beat and a simple *harmonic* pattern suggested by white vaudeville music, blackfaced minstrel music and hillbilly harmonica playing. The strange, disturbing hiatus between vocal and instrumental elements, typical of Barbara Dane's blues, has gone. This is still more the case in a typical rock 'n' roll performance, wherein the primitive blues has been metamorphosed into pop. Ray Charles's version of *Alabama Bound* is an excellent example. He preserves the blues inflection in pitch and rhythm, which gives the music its characteristic "lift," an intensity of feeling beneath the exuberance and bounce; we feel he knows what he's singing about when he tells us that he's banished the heebie-jeebies. Nonetheless, the drive of the music, scored for big band, is that of the powerhouse. The country blues, streamlined, seems to have entered the world of commerce.

Up to this point this tradition in pop music, stemming from a deliberate revival of the most primitive form of blues, has followed a predictable path, gradually increasing in sophistication and in technical expertise. With the appearance of the Beatles, however, something odd happens, which may not be unconnected with the fact that they are British, outside the main tradition of American pop culture. Rock 'n' roll music incorporated folk elements into conventions deriving from Tin Pan Alley, whereas the melodic, rhythmic and harmonic texture of the Beatles' songs is itself primitive; at least it has more in common with conventions of late medieval and early Renaissance music than it has with the harmonic conventions of the eighteenth century and after. Consider one of the Beatles' most celebrated songs, *She Loves You*. The key signature is the three flats beloved of pop convention; however, the opening phrase is pentatonic, or perhaps in an Aeolian C which veers towards E flat, and much of the effect depends on the contrast between the ascending sharp sevenths and the blue flat sevenths of folk tradition. Nor is the final chord of the song simply an added sixth cliché; or if that's what the guitar chord is, the melody suggests that C, not E flat, is the root. Again, *A Hard Day's Night,* the theme song from the Beatles' first film, has no conventional tonic-dominant modulations. Instead, it has a distinctively plagal, "flat" feeling, beginning with the dominant seventh of the subdominant. The tune itself is pentatonic until the chromatic extension in the final phrase (which doesn't alter the harmony), and the verse section depends entirely on alternations between the tonic and the chord of the flat seventh (between C and B-flat triads). After the double bar we have mediant substitutions for dominants, while the coda phrase alternates sharp thirds with blue flat thirds in a manner characteristic equally of the true blues, and of the fase relations of sixteenth- and seventeenth-century English music. None of these features would be found in post-eighteenth-century textbook harmony: the flat seventh-chord flourish in the guitar postlude is strikingly similar to passages in the keyboard music of Farnaby or Gibbons!

Of course this doesn't necessarily mean that the Beatles have ever heard, or even heard of, medieval or Renaissance music, any more than the peasant folk singer knew he was singing in the Dorian mode. It's rather that their melody and harmony, welling up in their collective subconscious, discovers authentic affinities with music of a relatively early, less "harmonic" stage of evolution, and thereby reinforces the primitivism of their rhythm. Even the noise of the electric guitar, though in part commercially dictated because of the sheer volume necessary to get across to vast audiences, emulates the "primitive" sound of the multi-stringed Blue Grass banjo, a white folk music. In their most recent discs (1965), the Beatles have, indeed, employed far more primitive instrumental techniques, imitating the guitar-picking styles of the most rudimentary country blues and using an electronic organ to suggest harmonica, bagpipes, jew's-harp and still more basic rural instruments. At first Ringo's use of an Indian sitar in place of banjo or guitar was no more than a pleasing new sonority applied to the Western-style tune *Norwegian Wood*. On their latest disc, however, the characteristic Merseyside electronic noises merge into sonorities and techniques that are specifically Eastern; and the Beatles couldn't do this so effectively if they were merely picking up fashions from the sophisticated world. There is a genuine connection between what is happening in pop music and what is happening in "art" music and in jazz. The remarkable song *Tomorrow Never Knows* begins with jungle noises very similar to Coleman's or Coltrane's "free" jazz, and employs both vocal and instrumental techniques which we may find both in Ornette Coleman and in Stockhausen! Interestingly enough, the words of the song tell us to "Turn off your mind; relax and float downstream: it is not dying. Lay down all thought; surrender to the voice: it is shining. That you may see the meaning of within: it is being." One couldn't wish for a more unequivocal abnegation of Western "conciousness"; and the disturbing quality of the music certainly suggests that we're not meant merely to take it ironically.

Naturally enough, the Mersey sound has been, at least in its earlier and cruder manifestations, commercially manipulated. Yet the impressive nature of their recent development suggests that it always was the spontaneity and authenticity of the Beatles' return to "beginnings" that has given their music, no less than their characters, its obsessive appeal, and has distinguished it from that of groups who have made a more conscious attempt to imitate primitive models. Moreover, it's interesting that when sophisticated composers such as Burt Bacharach produce pop numbers, they exploit knowingly the techniques which, in Beatle music, were instinctive. Bacharach's *Anyone Who Had a Heart,* made famous by Cilla Black, uses the same mediant transitions and shifting sevenths as characterize the Beatles' songs. There are more of them, in somewhat more surprising relationships, but the principle is the same, and equally remote from post-eighteenth-century convention. Again, the tune itself has a pentatonic tendency, while the irregular groups of repeated notes suggest an affinity with folk monody, derived from the inflections of speech. Perhaps there's even a link with folk tradition in the words' and tune's simple, suffering, numbing resignation. It's the opposite pole to the Beatles' bounce, but it isn't, like the Stephen Foster–derived Tin Pan Alley ballad, self-pitying.

The intrusion of folk elements into the songs of a sophisticated pop composer like Bacharach hints that there may be a growing together of pop culture with the real folk-song revival movement: a hint which is reinforced by the recent phenomenal success of Bob Dylan. This American lad, after an abortive career at a provincial college, wandered the country with his guitar, a new-style hobo, writing and singing his own songs. Ray Charles, back in the days of rock 'n' roll, lustily sang, the Beatles boisterously shout, Bob Bylan rustily croaks; this apparent decline in musical significance, however, is accompanied by a progressive increase in verbal significance. Dylan writes his own words, which are always *about something,* usually of urgently topical and local import. Quite often these words are of poetic intensity, resembling real ballad poetry, the nursery rune, or even on occasions the songs of Blake; they have to be listened to, if the experience is to mean anything. Whereas a typical Beatle performance may be totally inaudible beneath the screams of appreciation, a similar mass audience of young things will listen to Bob Dylan in a silence in which the proverbial pin could be heard dropping. Attention presupposes a rebirth of consciousness. Bob Dylan's primitivism, in succession to the Beatles', may mean a new start.

Basically, Dylan's music is far more primitive than that of the Beatles, or even the Rolling Stones. *The Ballad of Hollis Brown,* for instance, tells a (true) story of the poor white who "lived on the outside of town, with his wife and five children and his cabin fallin' down." His baby's eyes look crazy, the rats get his flour, bad blood gets his mare, his wife's screams are "stabbin' like the dirty drivin' rain." He kills his family and himself with a shotgun, and the song ends, "There's seven people dead on a South Dakota farm. Somewhere in the distance there's seven new people born." The tune of this ballad could hardly be more primitive, for it is entirely pentatonic and most of the time is restricted to four notes, while the guitar part oscillates between the tonic and dominant. The restricted vocal range, the obsessive ostinato, have a dramatic function, suggesting the numbing misery of poverty; the deliberately antilyrical, dead-pan vocal production has a comparable effect, which is by no means merely negative and deflationary. The primal simplicity of the tune and accompaniment carries its own affirmation, even resilience. The end isn't nirvana; life goes on, however insignificant one's personal destiny.

In *Masters of War* Dylan uses a similarly nagging pentatonic tune and reiterated ostinato to build up a cumulative fury. But not all his songs are musically as primitive as this. His social-satirical protest songs more commonly derive from white hillbilly style, rather than from the Negro blues. *With God on Our Side* has a swinging arpeggiated tune in slow waltz rhythm; Dylan's hiccups and hiatuses, and the occasional melismatic twiddle, point the irony of the words, which tell the bitter story of American martial history: "O the history books tell it, they tell it so well, The cavalries charged, the Indians fell, The cavalries charged, the Indians died, O the country was young, with God on its side." The song goes down through the Spanish-American War and the two World Wars, with an especially biting melisma for the Second World War, after which "we forgave the Germans and we were friends, Though they murdered six million In the ovens they fried, the Germans now too Have God on their side." After stanzas about the Russians, chemical warfare and the atom bomb, the song reaches its climax: "In many a dark hour I've been thinkin' all this, That Jesus Christ was betrayed by a kiss. But I can't think for you, You got to decide, Whether Judas Iscariot Had God on his side." The guileless tune, and the harmonica ritornelli which seem to come from another Eden, make the savagery of the words the more trenchant; it's not surprising that even in an "affluent" society, young people listen to Dylan croaking these words in an electrically tense silence.

In many of his songs Dylan adapts both the words and tunes of traditional folk ballads to contemporary ends. Thus, *A Hard Rain's Gonna Fall* is a version of Lord Randal: "O what did you see my blue-eyed son? I saw a new born baby with wolves all around it, I saw a highway of diamonds with nobody on it, I saw a black branch with blood that kept drippin', I saw a roomful of men with their hammers a bleedin', I saw a white ladder all covered with water," etc. *Who Killed Davy Moore?* transforms Cock Robin into an anecdote and parable about a calamity in the boxing ring, with social and political overtones. The mainly pentatonic tune is very fine, the words at once witty and scary, naturalistic yet with a flash of poetry when the boxer falls "in a cloud of mists." This isn't so far away from the authentic folk-revival tradition as represented by Joan Baez, who has her protest song *What Have They Done to the Rain?*, with its obsessive rhythmic ostinato, its plagal flatness which is possibly a mixolydian G. The fusion of pop and modern folk seems to be consummated when a Baez disc enters the Top Ten.

Many Bob Dylan tunes have been sung recently by folk singers such as Joan Baez, Odetta and Pete Seeger. The latter's version of *Davy Moore* is especially impressive, and interesting because he sings it not in Dylan's dead-pan, uninvolved manner, but with considerable passion. That he makes it a *dramatic* song-story is significant, since despite the Beatles' and Dylan's primitivism we know that the situation today isn't really the same as it was in primitive societies. Once having experienced knowledge and power, man cannot be entirely ignorant of moral choice; he's bound to ask, even if he's a pop artist dealing in myths rather than in personal expression, whether some myths aren't "better than" others. So the pop artist is inevitably an artist, once more making choices, using conscious techniques better or worse, *for* better or worse, as we can see from the Beatles, however spontaneous their creative origins may have been. What matters is how effectively he can learn to be reborn through the absorption of "preconscious" folk techniques, notwithstanding the commercial pressures he's submitted to.

Bob Dylan is said to be worried that he, the hobo troubadour, now nets an income of $500,000 a year. No doubt he is bearing up pretty well; if his art does so too, even as well as that of the Beatles, it may not be extravagant to say that youth's new world is winning through. In this context we should beware of the glib assumption that a capitulation to commercial techniques is necessarily a capitulation to commercial values. It's easy to say that Dylan's recent discs, employing electrically amplified guitar instead of the natural folk guitar and sometimes calling for the souped-up, big-band sound, corrupt his folk-like authenticity. Sometimes this is true, sometimes it isn't; and it is surely more, not less, "natural" for a folk singer living in an electronic age to exploit, rather than to spurn, electronic techniques. The folk purists are also the escapists; Dylan has proved that it is possible to be a myth-hero and an artist at the same time, and to carry the integrity of the rural folk artist into a world of mechanization.

There is thus a true parallel between a Dylan's desire for a rebirth, using not refusing the techniques of an industrial society, and the concern with a new birth of a Cage or a Feldman. It is interesting that the most insidiously haunting of all Dylan's songs should be a recent number, *Mr. Tambourine Man,* which, far from being a socially committed protest, looks superficially like an escape from life to dream. In a sense it is, for the tambourine man is a marijuana peddler; yet Dylan specifically says that he is "not sleepy," even though there ain't no place he's going to. Drug addiction is not, of course, itself a positive solution; but the song suggests that the impulses that have driven young people to it *could* have a positive outcome. We can sense this because the song is so beautiful. Like the tranced music of Cage or Feldman, it appeals for a different kind of commitment; it's a Pied Piper myth encouraging us to follow the unconscious where spontaneously it leads us, and this is most movingly suggested both by the wavery ballad-like refrain and also by the irregularity of the verbal and musical clauses which pile or float up, one after the other, like smoke rings. The metaphor of smoke rings actually appears in the verses which transport Dylan, a "ragged clown," beyond the "twisted reach" of sorrow. Release from the mind's tension, for Dylan no less than for Cage and Feldman, is a necessary step toward rediscovery; losing the self, in the ancient Biblical phrase, in order to find it, we are encouraged to forget "consciousness" today so that we may recharge our spiritual batteries for tomorrow. Such a pop song haunts us so disturbingly because its mythology plumbs unexpectedly deep; indeed, one might almost say that it not only links up with the extremism of Cage and Feldman, but also reminds us how the avant-garde has not been without effect even on the central, humanistic and Christian traditions of European music. Though this is unlikely to have been a matter of direct influence, it's an indication that, in Dylan's phrase, "the times they are a-changin'." In our final chapter, therefore, we must return to Stravinsky, to consider the later history of his retreat from humanism. Then we must discuss Benjamin Britten's two church operas as a fusion of old values with new. This will lead to a consideration of one of our younger composers, Peter Maxwell Davies, who is often loosely grouped with the avant-garde, though his music has affinities with traditions associated with both Stravinsky and Britten.

VII

Incarnation and Revelation: The Promise of the Future

If we accept Stravinsky as the most "central" representative of twentieth-century music, though not necessarily as the greatest twentieth-century composer, we have to admit that he is representative in a paradoxical way. For just as he has expressed himself through a deliberate denial of what we are accustomed to call expression, so he has been representative by turning his back on most of the values and assumptions that have made us what we are. This suggests that we, too, are at least subconsciously distrustful of the beliefs in which we have been nurtured. The Stravinskian dubiety is also ours: which matters because his art's admission of dubiety is more honest, less afraid, than most of us can hope to be.

We have examined the nature of this dubiety in discussing Stravinsky's early, neoprimitive works. The ritual in those works, though cathartic and beautiful, couldn't be true; we could only act it, not live it, which is why the ritual had to be incarnated in the conscious artifice of ballet. That Stravinsky himself was aware that the burden of consciousness cannot be brushed aside merely by a recalling of the primitive springs of life is suggested by the fact that, in wartime works such as *The Soldier's Tale,* the theme of human guilt and responsibility makes a somewhat queasy appearance in a puppet-like parody of the Faust legend. Techniques and conventions from widely separated bits of Europe's "humanist" past are disturbingly reintegrated, while the primitive element becomes a conscious sophistication of twentieth-century jazz. The queasiness, even the cynicism, were serious enough in purpose and effect, and had positive direction in that they led Stravinsky to explore, in the "neoclassic" works of his middle years, his relationship to the great humanist tradition. Like his Renaissance and baroque predecessors, he took his themes from classical antiquity, rather than from Christian tradition, for he did not wish, at this point, to be concerned with a dichotomy between spirit and flesh. He started from those conventions whereby men of the baroque world had conveyed their belief that Man might be Hero, even to the point of divinity. In effect, however, he inverted the significance that these conventions had had at the time when they were created. We can examine this process in Stravinsky's opera *Oedipus Rex,* perhaps the key work in his long career, and the only one to make *direct* use of the conventions of baroque opera, wherein the humanist attempted man's deification.

A real heroic opera—and this applies too to Handel's oratorios, which are heroic operas on Biblical subjects—was simultaneously a ritual of humanism (a masque or State ceremonial) and a drama dealing with the perversity of man's passions, which makes paradise-on-earth a difficult ideal. Stravinsky preserves the "heroic" closed aria form and also the atmosphere of ritual ceremony. At the same time he admits that we can hardly belong to this ritual, any more than we could share in the primitive ritual of *The Wedding.* He symbolizes this by returning to the (authentically Greek) stylization of the mask, and by having the opera acted and sung in a dead language (Latin), interspersed with narration in modern French. The narration is done by a man in modern evening dress (in the original performance by Cocteau himself, the librettist). This smart, nineteen-twentyish convention becomes, in the hands of a master at the height of his powers, unexpectedly moving. It tells us that we, like the narrator, are cut off from the springs of passion and from the humanist's celebration; then gradually, as the tragedy unfolds, we come to realize that it is our tragedy after all. We may not be kings, great or noble as is Oedipus, but we too are subject to the destiny that hounds us; and it is only our pride that prevents us from seeing that destiny is the guilt within us all. From this point of view it is significant that Stravinsky chose, for this central work in his career, a myth that the more buoyant humanists of the heroic age had preferred to leave alone. For one thing, in its Freudian aspects, the myth stressed man's guilt, inherent in the fact of his birth; and Heroic man, though he made art out of the possibility of human error, was reluctant to admit that guilt could sully his divine pretensions. For another thing, the Oedipan myth contained another, immensely ancient strand, in which the theme of incest was less important than the revolt against patriarchal society, a desire to return to the embracing love of an earth goddess, Demeter. She was irrational, below consciousness, directly in touch with the magical mysteries. The theme we have repeatedly returned to throughout this book was already implicit in Stravinsky's opera, which deals directly with the ego's pride and also with the ego's insufficiency; and which links this insufficiency both with the "primitive" magic of his early works and with the mystical ritual of his later quasi-liturgical pieces.

After the spoken Prologue, in which Cocteau recounts the story in modern French, the chorus, masked like living statues, sing of the plague that ravages Thebes. They are the men of the city, but also Mankind, whose burden of suffering is a burden of guilt. The anti-expressive syllabic recitation, the ostinato patterns over chugging, B flat minor thirds, have affinities with Stravinsky's primitive phase, yet the effect is not one of orgiastic excitement. Indeed, falling minor thirds have always been a musical synonym for the domination of earth and therefore of death (consider the late works of Brahms); the feeling here is of almost claustrophobic constriction, of a submission to fate that may be equated with submission to death. Although we are not as yet aware of the significance of the twofold relationship, we sense, as we listen, that this music is complementary both to the primitive pieces and to the Christian liturgical works that, at this time, Stravinsky was composing for the Russian Orthodox Church.

In this grand, static lamentation there is virtually no harmonic movement, though there is much harmonic tension, created mainly by the telescoping of tonic, dominant and subdominant chords. There is a hint of very slow momentum as the chorus, in increasingly disjointed rhythm over nagging thirds, call on their King, Oedipus, to help them. Then, out of the prison of the falling thirds a prancing, dotted-rhythmed phrase is generated, and Oedipus, a high heroic tenor, sings in ornate coloratura, "Ego Oedipus"—I, Oedipus, will free you. Although the coloratura suggests the sublime assurance of the god-king, and derives from the ornamentation of Baroque opera, there is also a quality, in the high register and the oscillations around a fixed point, that reminds us of liturgical incantation. And Oedipus's freedom seems to be itself imprisoned, not only by the nodal oscillations of his vocal line, but also by a slowly revolving ostinato in the bass that chains down the clarinets' prancing arpeggios and reasserts the B flat minor obsession, against the voice's aspiration to C. Indeed, the fateful minor thirds continue intermittently, and are fully re-established in the *Serva* chorus, in which the men of Thebes ask their leader what is to be done that they may be delivered.

Oedipus says that Creon, the Queen's brother, has just returned from Delphi, where he has been to consult the oracles. Immediately, the B flat minor obsession is banished. Sonorous G-major chords from the chorus welcome Creon in hopeful luminosity; as they become ordinary men, looking toward their potential everyday activities, their music loses its monumentally tragic quality and becomes somewhat primitively Moussorgskian, for they, like us, are not kings. Creon, being at this stage a representative of the gods, sings a strict *da capo* aria, in which there can be no development since perfection is unalterable. But there's a certain ambivalence in his music, as there was in the heroic aria of the Baroque age itself. The middle section of the aria, touching on F minor, hints at the B-flat-minor obsession as it refers to the old, dead king, while there is something frenzied about the C-major assertiveness of the aria itself. The widely arpeggiated tune is crude, even cruel, with the brass-band vigor of early Verdi rather than the grandeur of Handel, and the rhythmic ostinato on four horns suggests a preconscious terror beneath the surface. The man-god complacence carries all before it, however. After he has informed the chorus that the oracles report that the murderer of their former king Laius is among them and must be discovered, Creon concludes with a tremendous C-major arpeggio: *Apollo dixit deus.*

Oedipus, as leader, responds to the challenge. He boasts of his skill in solving riddles, which stands as a symbol of man's ability to control his destiny through reason, and promises to save his people by discovering the murderer. This aria, which is in E flat (the opera's man key, as opposed to C major, which is the key of the gods), is an almost hysterical intensification of his earlier ornate style. Beginning with prideful, arpeggiated phrases which emulate those of Creon, it turns into more emotionally agitated sevenths, emphasizing in tipsy narcissism the word "ego" as it sweeps into oscillating coloratura. Over the sustained E-flat bass the voice resolves the fourth on to the prideful major third, but although the music is superb in the strict sense, the chorus seem to suspect that there is something a little phony about it. Their reiterated "deus dixit tibi" phrase is metamorphosed back into the fateful minor thirds, now screwed up a semitone into B minor. After invoking the gods Minerva, Diana, Phoebus and Bacchus, they call on Tiresias, blind prophet who sees in the dark, since he would be more likely to help them than a human leader, however mighty. In liturgically solemn, repeated notes and widespread arpeggio figurations, oscillating tonally between Man's E flat and God's C major, Tiresias says that he will not, cannot, reveal the truth. Oedipus, his imperturbability threatened, taunts Tiresias: whereupon, in a line of immense, superhuman range, Tiresias announces that the king's murderer is a king. For the first time the tonality hints—by way of a C-major–A-minor ambiguity that merges into G—at D major, with a resonant triad on horns reinforced by double basses in octaves.

At the moment we don't realize the significance of this, for Oedipus takes over the sustained D natural, only to force it back to his man key of E flat. Yet though Oedipus has been ruffled by his encounter with Tiresias, it marks a stage in his spiritual pilgrimage, and his second E-flat aria is only superficially similar to the first.

Though the line is derived from his "superb" aria, it is now broken, chromatic, even fragmentary. For the first time he reveals his weakness, which is also his humanity, accusing Creon and Tiresias of plotting against him, bragging of his abilities as riddle solver and appealing to the chorus not to forget his previous triumphs. His proud line now carries harmonic implications that imbue it with pathos, even tenderness. Significantly, he ends unaccompanied, singing the *chorus's* falling minor thirds, and in C minor, relative of E flat and halfway to the god key which is C major. In seeing himself as one with the many he proceeds from pride to humility; he begins, tremulously, hesitantly, to accept fate and death in his music, if not in his words. It is interesting that, formally, this song is not a *da capo* aria, but a rondo in which the episodes change the destiny of the theme. His absolutism disintegrates, even while he tries to assert it. This is why the act can conclude with a Gloria, celebrating Jocasta's arrival in Stravinsky's "white note" diatonicism. The personal life of Oedipus's rondo-aria is banished; the ceremonial music that succeeds is related more to Stravinsky's music for the Russian Orthodox Church and even to his primitive works than to the harmonic ceremonial of a heroic composer such as Handel. Indeed, the chorus strikingly anticipates the *Symphony of Psalms.*

Oedipus's rondo-aria, which has more harmonic movement than any previous music in the opera, and the consequent Gloria, which has no harmonic movement at all, together make the axis on which the work revolves. The Gloria concludes the first act, and is repeated as prelude to the second, which follows the path to self-knowledge. To begin with, Jocasta pours scorn on all oracles. Her music hasn't the rigid, frigid panache that comes of Oedipus's desire for self-deification; it has a human, almost Verdian, lyrical sweep and a harmonic momentum such as Oedipus acquires only in his rondo. The key, G minor, is dominant of the godly C, relative of the fateful B flat; her reiterated syncopations and chromatic intensifications suggest an essentially human defiance. Defiance, in the F-major middle section of the *da capo* form, turns into insolent ridicule. To chattering clarinet triplets she points out how oracles often lie, and must do so in this case, for the old king was killed twelve years ago, outside the town, at the crossroads. The repeated eight-note figuration sounds panic-stricken, however; and when the *da capo* returns the syncopations and chromatics affect us differently, seeming to be dragging and anguished rather than defiant. At this point we realize that the minor thirds pad unobtrusively beneath the impassioned lyricism. She too struggles against destiny; and if, being a woman, she is more immediately human than Oedipus, she is also less heroic, and is not, like him, absolved.

Oedipus's assurance is finally shaken by Jocasta's reference to the past, for he recalls that twelve years ago he killed a stranger at the crossroads. Hypnotically, the chorus takes up the word "trivium," hammering it into Oedipus's mind. "Ego senem kekidi," he stammers, to a phrase that inverts the falling thirds, accompanied only by terrifying C-minor thirds on the timpani. This is the moment of self-revelation, when he sees that the guilt is within. At first the revelation leads to chaos, only just held in check by the rigidity of the ostinato pattern. Jocasta screams in wild 12/8 chromatics that the oracles always lie, while Oedipus sings in duo a strange, bewildered, broken lament, confessing his past history. So the mother-wife and the son-husband sing together, in C minor, relative of the man key E flat, tonic minor of the god key C major. On this a B-flat ostinato closes remorselessly, as Oedipus says that, though afraid, he must know the truth, must see the shepherd who was the only witness of the crime.

An anonymous messenger, agent of destiny, enters to reveal that Oedipus's reputed father, Polybus, has died, admitting that Oedipus was an adopted son. The messenger, being a low, unheroic character, sings a Moussorgskian peasant-like incantation, oscillating around a nodal point. The chorus takes up the words "falsus pater," stuttering, horror-struck; words, line, and rhythm are all broken, the harmonic movement gelid. Momentarily, when the messenger tells them that Oedipus was found as a baby on Mount Citheron, with his feet pierced, the chorus sing in modal innocence that a miracle is about to be revealed: he will prove to be born of a goddess. But the shepherd witness comes forward to reveal the truth. In a swaying arioso that, like Oedipus's *kekidi* phrase, inverts the falling thirds, he carries the music back to the obsessive B-flat minor. The shepherd's aria, accompanied only by two bassoons and then timpani, induces a state of trance in everyone except Jocasta who, now knowing that she is the wife of her own son, who was his father's murderer, rushes out.

Oedipus thinks, or pretends to think, that Jocasta has gone off in shame at the discovery of his lowly birth. He makes a desperate return to his early arrogance and sings a scornful Italianate aria over a bouncing bass. The key, F major, is the same as the insolent middle section of Jocasta's first aria, and perhaps it is not an accident that F is the dominant of fate's B flat. But the human impulse to dominate is frantic now, as is suggested by the jaunty vivacity of the dotted rhythm that takes us back to Oedipus's first appearance. The coloratura has here a kind of horrifying inanity, as though Oedipus is trying to cheer himself up, against all odds. The aria concludes in a cadenza of hysterical exultation, in wild descending chromatics that carry us, however, from F major to D minor. At this point the thudding minor thirds return, along with the hammering *kekidi* rhythm, and we realize that his exultation, though a mask, has not been entirely synthetic. Messenger, shepherd and chorus declaim the truth on repeated D's; woodwind and strings alternate to the *kekidi* rhythm in false relations between D major and minor; and Oedipus chants a brief arioso which, beginning in B minor over the pedal D's, miraculously transforms the falling minor thirds into D major on the words "lux facta est." Light floods his spirit as he decides to put out the light of his eyes; and like Shakespeare's Gloucester in *King Lear* he could say "I stumbled when I saw." So Stravinsky stresses the Christian implications that he can discover in the myth, and it is relevant to note that Oedipus's final arioso is closer to liturgical chant than it is to the heroic music he has sung previously. Or rather one could say that at the end he rediscovers the music that was implicit in his first utterance, which is now purged of egoism and self-will.

The transformation of the falling thirds into D major is the fulfillment of Tiresias's prophecy, which had also ended with a D-major triad. Then the triad had been immediately contradicted by Oedipus's E-flat egoism; now it is Oedipus himself who initiates the miraculous metamorphosis. The opera is dominated by the search for D major, which is the key of the inner light, and the tonal scheme of the work has a symmetry that is simultaneously musical and doctrinal. One can notate this in a kind of cyclical chart:

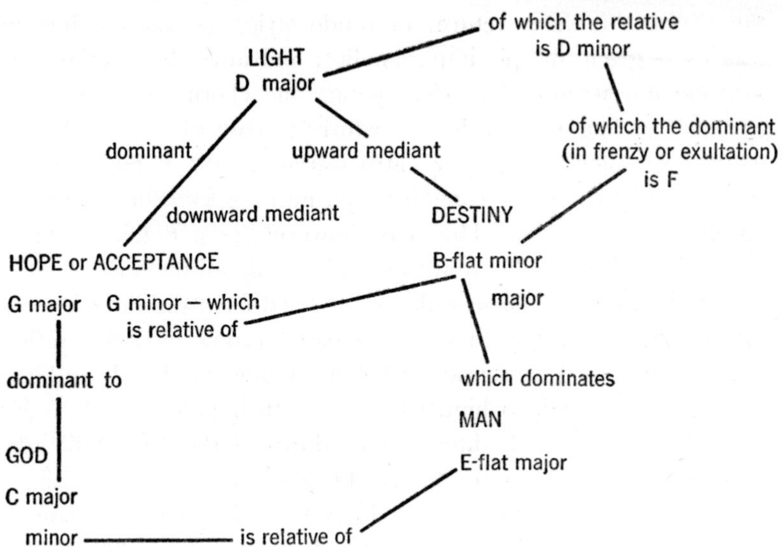

Stravinsky adheres to this scheme with consistency, and that he almost certainly did so without conscious intent emphasizes how instinctively he thinks and feels in ritualistic and "doctrinal" terms. The discovery of Light is the consummation of the tragedy, but an epilogue is needed to place the revelation in the context of our lives. So the visionary moment is followed by a trumpet fanfare in a tonally ambiguous region between B-flat major and G minor (see chart). The Messenger announces that Jocasta has hanged herself, and the chorus takes up his words, proceeding to tell us, in a sickening, lurching 6/8 rhythm, how Oedipus has blinded himself with a golden pin from her dress. The key is a compromise between C minor and E-flat major, for it is his and our humanity, not the moment of revelation, that we are concerned with now. The bass tends to oscillate around the E-flat pedal, but the vocal lines are tense with upward-thrusting chromatics and major-minor ambiguities. Significantly, the music refers back to the C-minor duo of horror and bewilderment that Oedipus and Jocasta had sung at the moment of discovery, for we know that we are involved in their doom.

After each phase of the narration of the suicide and self-blinding the trumpet fanfares return, in rondo style, so that the human tragedy is given an epic impersonality; and after each fanfare the instrumental texture that accompanies the chorus becomes more agitated, ending with scalewise, whirling sixteenth notes. On the words "spectaculum omnium atrocissimum," the C-minor–E-flat major ambiguity seems to resolve itself into a solemn brass cadence on the D-major triad. This acts, however, as a dominant to G minor, in which key the upward-shooting scales of the opera's opening are reinstated. (These scales are derived from the French overture of the heroic age, though they have become terrifying rather than pompously magisterial.) Oedipus totters in, blind, and the chorus says farewell to him, who carries their guilt as well as his own. Gradually the thudding minor thirds of the fate motif take over, now pulled down by the weight of sorrow from B-flat minor to G minor—dominant of the god key C, as B flat is dominant of the man key E flat. As the minor thirds fade out on cellos, double basses and timpani, the opera tells us that, though man is "dominated" by destiny, he may find his divine redemption. G minor is the relative of B flat, but also the gateway to light, which is D.

The Christian, rather than humanistic, implications of Stravinsky's heroic opera are fulfilled in the sequence of works that follows, most notably in the *Symphony of Psalms,* which has claims to be considered his masterwork. In this work he again starts from the baroque conventions of toccata and fugue. The similarity to baroque techniques, however, is no more than superficial, for the work shows little evidence of the baroque sense of harmonic momentum. Indeed, in so far as the themes tend to oscillate around a nodal point and the structures to be organized by linear and rhythmic pattern rather than by harmonic and tonal architecture, the *Symphony* is strictly comparable with some aspects of medieval technique, and the seemingly preordained or "doctrinal" system of key relationships is also in principle, if not in practice, appropriate to an age of faith. And here, in the marvelous lyrical expansion of the last movement, the faith is fulfilled, the music being at once an evocation of "the chime and symphony of Nature," and an act of worship.

The third phase of Stravinsky's career was already implicit in the *Symphony of Psalms,* which was, in turn, inherent in *Oedipus Rex.* This third phase begins with works such as the *Mass* and the *Cantata* wherein, starting from medieval texts, he consciously borrows medieval techniques also: the nonharmonic, nodal ostinato, the preordained, "doctrinal" serialism. His final acceptance of Webern's complete chromatic serialization is a logical extension of this neomedieval serialism. It has been frequently pointed out that Stravinsky does not employ his rows in a Webernian spirit but in a more literal sense, in much the same way as a medieval composer used his cantus firmus as the Word. The difference, of course, lies in the fact that the cantus firmus did have doctrinal significance which was intelligible to at least a fair proportion of the people who listened to the music. Stravinsky's Word, on the other hand, is a private invention, and since we do not live in an age of faith we cannot participate in a ritual, or at least not on the terms in which it is offered to us. One may question, too, whether Stravinsky's music has ever again achieved the lyrical fulfillment it reaches in the *Symphony of Psalms.* That work, which is certainly among the two or three supreme masterpieces of the twentieth century, is a revelation of God's love because the creator attains, in the last movement, to the love of God. In comparison, Stravinsky's later works seem to be in love with the idea of God, rather than with God Himself, and in this too he may well be "representative." There hasn't been a great religious composer since (in their different but complementary ways) late Beethoven and Bruckner; one would hardly expect such a composer, in the world we have made. Nonetheless, the great, central composers of our time have been seekers. Schoenberg, starting from an awareness of chaos and disintegration both within the psyche and in the external world, thought of himself as a Moses who tried, but failed, to lead his people into the Promised Land; Stravinsky, in *Oedipus Rex* and the *Symphony of Psalms,* admitted to the humanist's burden of guilt and had his momentary vision of redemption. In both cases, the creator started from man-as-he-is.

If a criticism seems to be implied in the previous paragraph, it is not a criticism of Stravinsky, any more than it's a criticism of Schoenberg to speak, as we did, of his failure. There is a deep allegorical significance in the fact that Stravinsky, our spokesman, should be in a sense a composer of denial. We know that although the rite has not always been, with him, an act of revelation, it has been a historical necessity. Like Webern, another composer who has sought revelation through denial, he came to accept as historical necessity the fragmentation of line and the disintegration of rhythm. Like Webern again, he must know too that something similar has occurred before in European history, at the expiring twilight of the Middle Ages, and that these late medieval linear and rhythmic contortions now seem grotesque rather than life-enhancing. They were not the creative essence of the Middle Ages, which had expressed supremely in Gregorian chant the fundamental human instinct for flow and continuity, following the heartbeat, but aspiring to an air-borne ecstasy. Yet the later dislocations were a "necessity," as was the imposition of an ever more rigid external authority, if we were to be rescued from chaos. Doubtless the twentieth-century dislocations are necessary, too; certainly we cannot doubt the probity of Stravinsky's "authority," even though, being man-made rather than god-given, its purpose and destiny are obscure. And we listen with the deeper respect because we remember that Stravinsky has shown us, especially in the work of his middle years, that even in our bruised and battered world the heart may still sing in the sustained lyrical period, the pulse beat in a rhythm that is not motorized, but fluid and compulsive as the sea. When it happens, it is both true and miraculous, for Stravinsky's "representative" significance lies in the fact that he is not by nature a lyrical composer.

Benjamin Britten is—too easily so, Stravinsky would probably maintain, though it's perhaps inevitable that the two most materially successful composers of our time should regard one another with a degree of suspicion. Those of us who consider both Stravinsky and Britten to be great composers (if less great than a Bach or Beethoven) may recognize that the key theatrical works in their respective careers are complementary. Stravinsky's *Oedipus* transmutes humanism, by way of an oriental abnegation, into a Christianity reborn; Britten's two church operas, *Noye's Fludde* and *Curlew River,* start from Christian assumptions, but use their medieval and oriental techniques to purge the Christian heritage of guilt. Both the Stravinsky and the Britten works represent a fusion of West and East, and in both cases the fusion is re-creative, not evasive.

Britten began his career with a rebirth, a work specifically called *A Boy Was Born,* written when he was still a boy himself. Despite the archaism of the texts and of some of the musical procedures, the essence of this work is its theatrically re-creative immediacy; a boy is born indeed, and in the thirty years that have followed Britten has never forgotten that Boy and Birth. The wonderful Hardy songs deal directly with the birth of consciousness which is also the death of innocence, and almost all his operas have the same theme. The limitation of range is part of the evidence of his genius, for in dealing with innocence and persecution he knows what he knows. The relevance of the theme of the sacrificial scapegoat to our time is clear enough: we are obsessed with innocence because we have lost it, and because we have lost it we persecute those who haven't.

The grandest statement of this motif is in Britten's first opera, *Peter Grimes.* The unhero is here a genuinely tragic figure: the Savage Man who, given different circumstances, might have grown to civilized consciousness. Deprived of love, however, he destroys the Boy who is his own soul, and is hounded to his death by the World. Similarly, *Billy Budd* is specifically about the agony of growing up. Billy is a child destroyed by his childishness, which becomes the *mea culpa* of his stammer; the opera tells us that we can't dispose of evil by a blind blow, provoked by the inarticulateness of the good within us. Among the chamber operas, *The Rape of Lucretia* introduces an overtly Christian note into its fable of innocence corrupted, and *Albert Herring* has the same theme, almost the same story, as *Grimes,* but with a comic instead of tragic apotheosis. *The Turn of the Screw* offers Britten's most direct and painfully involved statement of the childhood and corruption motif, while in *A Midsummer Night's Dream* it finds perhaps its most maturely resolved form.

All this being so, it is hardly surprising that Britten should, throughout his career, have devoted time to the creation of music for children, nor that his most extended children's piece, *Noye's Fludde,* should deserve to rank among his supreme achievements. The choice of a text itself, as so often with Britten, is evidence of genius, of a self-knowledge that finds what is needful for each occasion. Thus, the Chester Miracle Play is medieval and the common people with whom it deals are, despite the *intellectual* sophistication of medieval civilization, childlike at heart. On the other hand, the story is unambiguously a conflict, so that the piece can grow from (Orffian) ritual into music-drama, if not into full-fledged opera. Indeed, it starts from a direct admission of "humanistic" contrarieties; the congregation, including you and me, sing the well-known hymn "Lord Jesus think on me." This hymn is an appeal to Christ to restore to us purity and innocence, which if we're adult we've lost, or if we're children we're about to lose, in traveling through "darkness," "perplexity" and the Flood. We *start,* that is, with the consciousness of sin and earth-born passion, which we have to encompass before we can see "eternal brightness." Although the Flood is in one sense a destructive force, it is in another sense (as it was in Biblical myth) a necessary return to the unconscious waters.

So Britten sets the hymn as a rather wild march, a song of pilgrimage in which the pilgrims are the children, as well as everyone else who may be present in the church. The hymn's descending scale becomes a motif of affirmation ("think on me") throughout the opera, but the bass's mingling of perfect, god-like fourths and fifths with the devil's imperfect ones imparts a slightly savage flavor to the simple diatonic harmonies. The devilish, bitonal F naturals initiate the conflict—between good and evil, between guilt and redemption—which the drama is. When, in the third stanza, the words refer directly to the Flood, the harmonies become more chromatic. Possibly Britten intends these rather corny harmonies to remind us of the turnover in the stomach and the chill down the spine that the reverberating organ gave us, in the parish church, when we were young. Possibly it still does the same, for children who go to church; in any case, it tells them, as it reminds the grownups, of the Flood they must pass through, to reach maturity.

This is manifest at the start of the opera's action, for the congregational chorale introduces the Voice of God who declaims (not sings) over fourths that are both perfect and imperfect. He may be the maker of all things, but man, through the sin and guilt that Orff's pagan music has no knowledge of, has thrown God's blessings away. The theme of redemption is then introduced, because mankind may be saved through the agency of Noah's Ark, which will breast the Flood. Noah, who is Man, sings to summon his children to an act of work and worship. The modal E minor of the hymn (which we may think of as the key of pilgrimage) changes to a pentatonic simplicity, full of godly fourths and optimistic major thirds and sixths. This leads into a work song as everyone gathers for the building of the Ark: an Orff-like music of ritual action which becomes drama. The dancing tune which Noah's children sing is derived from his original call, and is still pentatonically innocent, at once medieval and jazzy in its syncopated rhythm, marvelously suggesting youth's equivocal eagerness and apprehension. So even in music as simple as this there is theatrical projection and character portrayal; while the rapid modulations, or rather shifts of key, are also a dramatic device to convey excitement. Similarly, a primitive contrapuntal ensemble becomes a vivid musical image for corporate action; this music is inseparable from physical gesture and mime, which is one reason why children enjoy performing it. Suddenly and dramatically, the music breaks off, at what seems to be a climax of solidarity, when everyone is about to work together, hammering and sawing and caulking to make the Ark that will save us all.

What disrupts this collective helpfulness is indeed the snake in the grass, the fly in the ointment. Sex rears its lovely head as Mrs. Noah, singing major sixths (D sharps) that create sensual (Wagnerian!) ninth chords, refuses to play any part in the labour of salvation. Instead, with her gossiping cronies, she breaks into a parody of the work song in rapid 6/8 tempo. Of course she's a comic character, but Britten's music makes evident that the attempt of the Middle Ages to laugh away the dualism of sex didn't lessen its impact. Noah tries to assert his authority, making one of the stock medieval jokes about shrewish wives. He doesn't expect her to take any notice, and in fact she disassociates herself from the building by sitting, with her gossips, at the side of the stage. The key abruptly changes from Mrs. Noah's mingled F-sharp minor and A major to F natural, and Noah initiates the building "in the name of God." The building song begins with God's rising fifths and is supported on an ostinato of fifths as bass, alternating between tonic and flat seventh. There is virtually no modulation, because this is ritual rather than drama. As a refrain between each stanza, however, Noah's children refer to the coming of the Flood, singing in four-rhythm instead of the ritual's triple pulse, and in increasingly full, emotionally involved harmonization which changes the F-major ostinato to minor. In this action-ritual, children are involved instrumentally, playing open strings on violins and twiddles on recorders while the ostinato pattern is repeated; this beautifully suggests how the act of work and worship concerns us all, through the ages.

When the Ark and the action song are finished, Noah invites his wife, the perennial Outsider, to come in. She refuses, in a line that is more humanistically energetic than her husband's. In a canonic chase she parodies Noah's words which, to medieval people, seems not far from blasphemy, and is enough to provoke God to a second utterance. He orders Noah to take the creatures into the Ark, two by two, and little boys summon them with a fanfare of bugles. Again, Britten exploits, imaginatively, the music of our everyday lives. The first congregational hymn had been a noise such as we've heard in church, time out of mind; similarly, the bugle procession is a noise we can hear in the streets on a Sunday morning, a noise in which our own Willies and Johnnies may well participate. The march, in the bugle key of B flat, is all tonic, dominant and sub-dominant, and reflects with realistic authenticity (like the marches in the music of Ives) the tang and tingle of the noise we'd actually hear, wrong notes and all. Of course the wrong notes are right, because part of the innocence, and it is right too that there should be no modulation, which the bugles' simplicity cannot accommodate, apart from a brief shift to D flat for some of the wilder creatures ("beares, woulfes, apes and weyscelles").

Between each statement of the march tune various beasts and birds emit Kyries of praise and thankfulness (oscillating simply between the fifth and fourth). The creatures are "natural" but not "conscious," so there is a kind of celestial farce in the bugle march and the squeaking of mice and gibbering of monkeys. Only when Noah and his children and their wives (representing Mankind) join in a jubilant ensemble as they enter the Ark is there a change of mood and mode. The Kyries gradually grow from comedy to liturgical awe, from the rocking two-note figure into a beautiful pentatonic melisma. This melisma is rooted on G, which seems to be the key of harmony between man and God, and is the "relative" of the more disturbed E minor, which is the key of pilgrimage. There is no more than a touch of G major here; though when Noah once more orders his wife to come in "for feare lest that she drowne," he reminds her, and us, of the first hymn that had asked for Jesus's pity on our sinfulness. In apparent paradox, she too sings the same phrase in protesting that she "will not oute of this towne." But if there is Man's (and Woman's) stupid pride in her defiance, there is also a kind of courage. This may be why she is not finally beyond redemption; it's the Mrs. Noah in all of us that makes us human. Persistently, she sings sharpened sevenths against the hymn's modal flat sevenths. As humanist, she demands harmonic consummation, and throughout this dramatic exchange trills on a low D sharp (major seventh of E minor) repeatedly deny the tune its resolution into G. Mrs. Noah says to D-sharpish arpeggios over an E-minor triad, that she'd rather have her gossips than salvation, and sings, with the gossips, the Flood song, wherein the D sharps are aggressive over a lurching E-minor ostinato. Between the stanzas of the song, Noah tries to call her home, with the hymn's descending scale, to G major. But the D-sharp trills drive us back to the "lumpy," D-sharp-dominated ostinato. This, again, is an Orffian ritual piece that turns into drama.

The gossips say they'll sit there "regardless," and get drunk, their justification being the typically human imbecility that they "ofte times have done so." Habituation is all, and human pride becomes indistinguishable from hysteria. The sons take over from Noah, appealing to their mother in radiant parallel 6:3 chords, and with a humbly flattened, Phrygian version of the hymn phrase, drooping down to G by way of B flat and A flat. This flatness further counteracts the sharpness of Mrs. Noah's sevenths, and although her denials then grow frenzied, mingling D sharps with fiercer leaps and tenser intervals, she willy-nilly finds herself singing the hymn theme of redemption, as her sons bundle her into the Ark. She struggles, of course, and boxes Noah's ears, but the tide is turned and the hymn phrase sounds in fortissimo unison, not yet in the resolution of G major, but in the original E minor. With a sudden, miraculous shift to a sustained C-minor chord on the organ—a further subdominant flattening of the Phrygian G minor of the last reference to the hymn-tune, the D sharps finding rest in being metamorphosed into the E flats of the triad—Noah says that "it is good for to be stille." It is indeed, after the fury and the mire of human veins, and the stupidities of the human will; now the redeeming Storm can work its way.

The Flood takes the form of a passacaglia, with a chromatic, rhythmically restless theme in which a falling third expands to a fourth and then to a godly fifth, only to wind itself back to the original drooping third. Though it generates the storm's excitement, the passacaglia theme is also God's Law which is beyond change, and again the piece is action as well as music. The drama is epic, concerning not individual men, but man's fate through successive generations. Child recorder players and open-string fiddlers place the epic in its present context, as they emulate wind, waves and flapping rigging. The animals panic to rising and falling chromatics, until gradually everyone begins to sing, over and through the passacaglia, the hymn "Eternal Father, strong to save." This Victorian tune includes the falling scale figure of the first congregational hymn, but also a rising *chromatic* scale to express the urgency of our appeal to God. Britten manages to suggest that this chromaticism is both a part of our heritage (we've thrilled to it as long as we can remember), and at the same time something that has been discovered during the slow chromaticizing of the storm. The passacaglia bass persists as the congregation joins in the hymn, but disappears during a triumphant repetition with full organ and a descant of boy trebles. After we've achieved, with God's help, this victory over darkness, the storm can subside. The various storm incidents are heard in shortened form, in reverse order over the declining bass theme, now dominated by pedal G's on drums. The passacaglia closes in a profound calm, with an ostinato of spattering raindrops, played on suspended mugs and piano. The tonality is poised between G and the subdominant C.

We still don't know precisely what the calm signifies, nor does Noah, who sends out the Raven and the Dove, the black bird and the white, to spy out the land and the waters. The point of this Christian mythology would seem to be the interdependence of good and evil: only through the Raven is the Dove apprehensible, and we must pass through the Flood to attain redemption. The music for the two birds is, anyway, closely related. The Raven dances to a fast waltz, played on the humanly emotive cello; it is chromatically and rhythmically unstable, veering now this way, now that. There's an E-ish flavor to its tonality, for the Raven is still a pilgrim; yet his line is lyrically songful, and we hear the passacaglia theme again as he flickers off into the distance. This recollection of God's will carries the tonality flatwards toward the dominant sevenths of A flat. This hovers on the brink of G-major peace as the Dove, represented by flutter-tongued recorder, flies after the Raven in a graceful waltz that seeks to resolve the Raven's chromatics into rising diatonic scales. Tremulous dominant sevenths, repeatedly harking back to A flat, exquisitely suggest a mingling of ecstasy and awe, even fear, in the approach to G major bliss. When the Dove returns, alighting on the Ark, he brings our redemption in the shape of an olive branch; a transformed version of the passacaglia theme (in G with an E-ish flavor) becomes a melody, not a bass, while Noah sings simple but noble fourths and fifths as he tells us that "it is a sign of peace."

God's voice speaks quietly in forgiveness, bidding the creatures to go forth and multiply. Sleepily, the tonality sinks to a subdominant pedal C, reminding us of that earlier subdominant triad that made it "good for to be stille." Over the pedal C, the bugle-call key of B flat softly intrudes, and the animals and humans leave the Ark, two by two, singing B-flat alleluias. The syncopated theme reminds us of the first work song, of which it is, indeed, the spiritual consummation. Gradually, it is metamorphosed into a joyous ensemble, until the music changes back from drama to ritual, with tolling bells and modal flat sevenths accompanying God's benediction. G major finally comes into its own as the key of peace, uniting man with God in the last hymn, "The spacious firmament on high." This tune includes the first hymn's scale figure in rising, and in its original falling, form, both now in unsullied diatonicism. Ritual bells and bugles continue to sound in B flat, the major relative of G minor, which would seem to be Nature's (preconscious) key. They remain unaffected even when everyone sings Tallis's hymn in G-major canon, for the creatures are what they are, eternally unchanging in their relationship to God's cosmos, whereas Man alone can progress from E minor to G major. The final pages are magic ritual in the ringing of B-flat bells and the blowing of B-flat bugles, and at the same time are the end of a human drama in the final resolution into a quiet, low-spaced, infinitely protracted G-major triad.

What is here achieved in childhood experience is explored at adult level in Britten's later "parable for church performance," *Curlew River*. In a program note to the first performance Britten tells us that the seed of the work was sown when, in 1956, he witnessed two performances of the Japanese Noh-play, *Sumidagawa:*

"The whole occasion made a tremendous impression on me, the simple touching story, the economy of style, the intense slowness of the action, the marvellous skill and control of the performers, the beautiful costumes, the mixture of chanting, speech, singing which with the three instruments made up the strange music."

If he was to create a Noh-play himself, however, it would have to make contact with the Western world he lived in, and was heir to. How this might be possible was suggested by one of the odd coincidences that happen to genius.

For the Noh-play that Britten saw tells a tale that is close to Christian myth, and closer still to the personal myth that has dominated all Britten's work. A mother, desperate in grief, is searching for her lost son, slain by the barbarian; in a vision she sees him reborn. So Britten's myth of innocence, of persecution and of the sacrificial scapegoat, reappears, but with one significant difference. In *Peter Grimes* the hero is the Wild Man, the barbarian who, having lost love, destroys the boy who is his own innocence. But in *Curlew River* the persecutor doesn't even appear, his story being narrated retrospectively. The central characters are the suffering mother and the boy himself, who, in momentary vision, is restored from death. The duality of persecution and guilt is absolved.

The action is transferred from medieval Japan to an early medieval church in the English fens, which is justifiable, since English morality plays were probably performed in a style more comparable with a Noh-play than with naturalistic drama. We begin with ritual, with monks singing the plainsong hymn *Te lucis ante terminum*. The duality of harmony is thus rejected. This remains true throughout the work, since the instrumental and ensemble textures are monophonic or at most heterophonic, one part doubling another at the unison or octave, with occasional variations at the fifth or fourth, over slow (because numerically complex) patterns on percussion. When the monks have assumed the garments of the characters, the drama can begin. A Traveller asks the Ferryman to carry him across the river that divides the Western Country from the Eastern Fens—a symbol of separation and also, perhaps, of the division between flesh and spirit. Each character has certain (mostly stepwise) motives associated with him, and also his own instrument which, however, usually plays melismatic extensions of the vocal phrases. Thus, the Ferryman has a chromatically altered, agitated version of the plainsong theme, and the horn, thrusting or floating this melody across slow percussion, acts the gestures of rowing. The

Traveller, because he's traveling, covers more melodic space, though his Brittenesque thirds, accompanied by arpeggiated harp, tend to be stilled, rendered hieratic, by the infinitely slow reverberation of drone-chords on the chamber organ. Here and throughout the opera the chamber organ is used with magical inventiveness, in a manner comparable with the eternity-drone in both medieval and oriental music. While the Ferryman explains to the Traveller why people are gathering to celebrate the "special grace" of the boy's death, the chorus of monks sings the Curlew River's song of separation. Derived from the plainsong theme, in an undulating heterophony of parallel seconds, this reappears as refrain throughout the opera.

When the Mad Woman enters (sung by a man, with female mask), the music returns to a premedieval phase of consciousness, becoming pure line which is also gesture: song that merges into pathogenic speech, and into the glissando yell or sigh which are the heart's core. Her first phrase (perfect and imperfect fourth, and major seventh) is woman's grief, but also the curlew's call, here represented by flutter-tongued flute. Britten thus achieves an extraordinary equation between individual passion and universal lament. The instrumental line becomes a disembodied extension of the half-articulate cry that hurts too much to be borne; it's almost as though the woman's voice is her suffering humanity, and ours, while the flute is our yearning for spiritual grace. Only Janáček, among earlier opera composers, has used instrumental figurations as an extension of the voice's "gestures," though Britten's use of the technique is more radical, since he relies on nothing except line and rhythm. This is evident in the arioso where the Mad Woman tells the story of her loss and her pilgrimage from the Black Mountains. Her voice and its instrumental echoes stutter in septuplet repeated notes, fading into glissando moans, as she gropes back into the past. The Ferryman and chorus jeer at her, parodying her melodic gestures, but the savage mockery is silenced by the flute's metamorphosis of the woman's stutter into a song of lyrical longing. The curlew's cry, over a shimmering harp drone, becomes the Eternal Beloved and, prophetically, the lost boy. The Ferryman allows the Mad Woman to board his boat with the Traveller.

vibrato. The sound, like the medieval texts, is innocent; yet the tonal precariousness makes the line also fragile and forlorn, so that if the music induces an incantatory serenity, it also hints at the perils flesh is heir to, as we grow into "the pain of consciousness." It's about the Boy's birth and, like most avant-garde music, about the necessity for *our* rebirth. At the same time the nervosity of the line reminds us that we are, and the Boy was, born into a "world so wylde," and the sexual undertones of the poems' references to "bobs of cherryes," "balles," "pennys" and "tennys" are probably present in the music's harmonic texture too.

Compared with Orff, the homophonic part-song versions of the carols imply an embryonic consciousness. The parts move in a restricted compass and in very close harmony, revolving (like plain-chant) around nodal points; the tritonal tensions which they create are the more disturbing because the melodic phrases are, in themselves, so brief and simple. It's as though the music were half eager, half reluctant, to escape from the innocence of the monodic state, and this must be why children, growing through puberty, could recognize it as peculiarly their music. Being at once innocent and slightly painful and "lost," it is relevant to twentieth-century children and to all of us who need to rediscover the youth of the heart. This is why Davies's children's music (like Britten's) is inseparable from his adult music; he is justified in saying that the children's part of *O Magnum Mysterium* is completed only by the grown-up organ fantasia which, though more difficult, is not a different kind of activity. This helps us to understand why the Christian theme inherent in Davies's music is meaningful independently of his belonging to the, or to any, Church.

In his earlier "adult" works Maxwell Davies was apt to employ the serial processes he had learned from Webern in a somewhat doctrinaire spirit, though most of his early music has more in common with medieval cantus firmus and proportional meter than with Viennese chromaticism. He also followed the late medievalists in literally destroying semantic communication by splintering words into detached syllables, and if the "Gothic desperation" was the (squawking) swan song of the Middle Ages, Davies's early music, like that of Stockhausen and Nono, may be part of the swan song of post-Renaissance Europe. With him, however, it's also a case of *reculer pour mieux sauter;* it's significant that, despite the medieval affiliations of his work, he also passionately admires Monteverdi, who created an (operatic) *Musica Nuova.* Monteverdi musically initiated modern Europe, transforming the linear techniques of theocracy into the harmonic techniques of humanism. Davies worked the other way round, recreating harmony in lyrical and melismatic monody; yet the point is that harmony is not denied in the process, but rather intensified. The early music of Davies tended to be, in its jittery tenuity, inadequately auralized; in the beautiful *Leopardi Fragments,* however, he sets fragmentary words by a neurotic poet of Europe's decay to music which fuses medieval and primitive elements with techniques derived from Monteverdi. The new texture, at once rich and simple, is both regenerative and heart-assuaging.

The later works involving chorus and instruments, such as the *Veni Sancte Spiritus* (which is hardly a children's piece, though written for the remarkable Princeton High School choir), explore similar techniques on a more extended and impressive scale. Here we can see how serial and canonic devices are used not to destroy but to define a harmonic texture, as they were in early Renaissance polyphony. This is why the texture of the music, despite the intermittent fragmentation, seems to have more in common with Stravinsky's *Threni,* or even with the *Symphony of Psalms,* than with post-Webernian fashion. The elaborate mensural writing and the partiality for monodic writing, as in the ecstatically fine-spun cantilena of the "O lux beatissima," exist alongside, and often help to create, the increasing density of harmony. And while the music's quavery intensity is a product of our time, it becomes affirmative in total effect. The hiccuping alleluias admit muscle and sinew as well as spirit, inducing a joy related to that of the jazz break; the tender "Dulce refrigerium" uses doctrinal canon to attain harmonic resolution. In being a "middle path" composer as compared with Boulez or Stockhausen, Davies faces up to the problem of temporality, and to its human implications. His most recent large-scale work, the *Second Fantasy on an In Nomine of John Taverner,* is by modern standards a very long work. It makes a new sound, if one less startlingly new than that of Messiaen's *Chronochromie* or Boulez's *Pli selon Pli.* Beyond the newness, however, this sound has human significance as an unfolding of melody in time, a coruscation of lines and tensions, a precarious resolution of conflict. There's evidence here that the humanistic forms of an opera, on the all too human theme of betrayal which is inherent in Taverner's life, may be well within Davies's grasp. Such an opera would, one suspects, have affiliations both with *Oedipus Rex* and with *Curlew River,* and despite its ritualistic flavor would discredit the fashionable assumption that our humanity, which is all we have, isn't worth the having.

This is what one comes back to if one attempts to speculate about the future of music. We have seen that a part of the revolution in twentieth-century music has been a return to the unconscious and to levels of being that have affinities with those of primitive societies, and that this is probably a much more significant matter than a mere escape from our perplexities. Marshall McLuhan has suggested that just as the Elizabethans were poised between medieval religious, corporate experience and our modern individualism, so we "reverse their pattern by confronting an electronic technology which would seem to render individualism obsolete and corporate interdependence mandatory." Our ordinary perceptions and habits of behavior are being remade by the new media, and we are finding the process both painful and chaotic because our heritage is of little help to us in dealing with the oral and aural (rather than literate and visual) civilization which may be latent in the new technology. Modern physics envisages a simultaneously existent past, present and future in which human consciousness may be the only moving element; and the modern physicist may have more in common with religious, medieval man, with the mystics of oriental cultures, with the alchemists and even with the magicians of primitive societies, than he has with the post-Renaissance rationalist. In considering composers from Debussy to Stockhausen, we have noted that artists have for years been intuitively aware of how radical a change this is.

If most of us have failed to grasp the nature of our metamorphosis, the reason may be that the visual chronology of Renaissance tradition has tied us to the conception of a historical past. This was irrelevant to primitive oral cultures, and may be equally so to our future.

The world is becoming a smaller place as our awareness of "space" grows larger; we can no longer think of our Western arts as autonomous. Developments in pop music cannot be isolated from what is happening in "serious" music, and the West's veering toward the East and the primitive can be understood only as complementary to the East's need of the West. The future of civilization is inseparable from what happens to, for instance, the emergent African nations, and this is as true in musical as it is in social and political terms. At one level the Africans' conflict between their indigenous traditions and their desire to catch up with Western Europe seems incapable of resolution. The ancient musical traditions (which we call primitive because they are nonharmonic, though they are rhythmically far more complex than ours) belong to an aural and oral culture and can have no valid relationship to the literate traditions of the West. Their attempts to pretend that they have a past and present comparable with ours thus tend to end in unconscious comedy or bathos, for their mock-Bartók (or mock Stravinsky, Webern or Berio) pieces sound jejune compared not only with the real thing, but also with their own native music. Yet one can understand the motives that prompted these inexpert, pseudo-sophisticated imitations: it is no longer adequate, or even relevant, for African composers, living in their new macadamed cities, to create tribally functional music in the old sense.

One can, however, pertinently point out that the new African art composers may be on the wrong tack; and can indicate positively that there is another aspect of Western culture—jazz and pop—which might have a more authentic relationship to African traditions. This isn't merely because there's an African fundament to what has become a Western art, but also because jazz and pop, being improvised and performing rather than notated musics, have affinities with an oral rather than literate culture. The admirable series of recordings made by Hugh Tracey for the African Music Society demonstrates how a generation of often highly skilled, virtuosic performer-composers is arising who exploit, with charm and vigor, the natural affinities between the music on which they were nurtured in their village, and the "commercial" music which radio and television have brought to their changing world. Similarly, an African jazzman such as Dollar Brand, in spontaneously fusing traditional African and Cape Coloured music with the Chinese, Moslem, Indian, European and American music heard in the streets, has created a musical eclecticism that breaks the barriers between classical, jazz and pop music, as well as between races. In musical significance the achievements of these men far exceed those of any African composer of "art" music; and the music tends to be best when the merging of traditional African elements into modern beat is closest. It is no longer possible to segregate the elements of African tradition—white hymnbook harmony, Negro gospel shout, primitive piano boogie, Italianate opera, pop beat. This may have bearing not only on the history of music, but in a wider sense on the story of twentieth-century civilization.

For it is not only the "emergent" consciousness that learns. We in Europe, we have seen, may be recovering some of the qualities of a primitive civilization, learning to live, as J. C. Carothers has put it, in the implicit magic, charged with emotion and drama, of the oral word; and it is not fortuitous that Carl Orff is reluctant to allow children to begin musical studies in his school if they have already learned to read and write. This is not because reading and writing are to be deprecated, but because first things must come first; indeed, in rediscovering the "rite words in rote order" we should remember that James Joyce's revoking of our remote, Finn-like, fishy, calibanistic ancestry is also a Wake and awakening. Our reborn primitivism has to contend with, not to evade, consciousness; having thrown up a Shakespeare or Beethoven, we cannot pretend they never existed. It is significant that one of the most "central" traditionalists of our time, Bartók, should have affiliations equally with the static "present" of Debussy and with the Becoming of Beethoven. Similarly, if "statistical" serialism and coin-throwing chance seem equally to discredit the human, they are balanced by a Boulez's or a Stockhausen's attempt to preserve human impulse within the relativity of time-space, and by indeterminacy which can be, in Boulez's words, "a liberation from robotism in an oppressed creative universe, weighed down by the petty abuses of power."

From this point of view our latter-day history is perhaps already implicit in the Orpheus myth which, we observed in our first chapter, had so obsessive an influence on Renaissance man. It was man's power, through his arts, to affect, even to control, Nature that was celebrated in the first phase of the story. The second phase looks like an extension of the first in that, through his arts, man seeks to conquer even Time and death, reversing the gods' decree. There is, however, another strand in this part of the tale, whereby Euridice becomes not only a representative of the social world and of marriage, but also an earth-goddess (Persephone, Demeter?) whom Orpheus can find only by entering the dark labyrinth. She may even merge into the Eternal Beloved, the anima to his animus, a part of the search for a human "wholeness" which his *looking back* betrayed. For his betrayal he is, in the third phase of the myth, torn to pieces by the Maenads; the White Goddess has been metamorphosed into the Terrible Mothers. The Mother Goddess is pre-Oedipal, a legacy of our infantile history, "unboundedly good," in Ian Suttie's phrase, to the young child, yet also "utterly terrible, in that her displeasure is the end of all good things and of life itself." Even so, Orpheus's dismembered head sings on, prophesying to the winds: an image which seems peculiarly relevant to the artist of our time, who has undergone a comparable dark pilgrimage.

Yet this is not an entirely adequate image for the modern artist; whether or not we still live in a Christian civilization, we cannot escape the implications of our Christian heritage. The matriarchal cultures fell before the aggression of the guilt-ridden religions which "must needs atone for sin and propitiate the outraged father by compelling others to worship him." So although Christianity had garnered much of its mythology from pagan sources that had stressed human wholeness (which linguistically has the same root as haleness and holiness), it came increasingly to emphasize division at the expense of unity. Into its preconscious Eden it introduced the duality of sex and of choice. Whereas in pre-Christian cultures the White Goddess and the Terrible Mother had been accepted as complementary faces of the same life-instinct, Eden's serpent, twined around the Cross, became a means toward consciousness. To be conscious is to be aware of difference—between self and not-self, life and death, love and hate, flesh and spirit. Only through the war of Cain and Abel, and of Esau (the hairy one of the earth) and Jacob (the hairless one of the spirit) can we hope to achieve again wholeness in union with God. In so far as the new primitivism, whether as manifested in the work of Boulez, Cage and Stockhausen, of Britten and Stravinsky, of Ornette Coleman, or of the Beatles and Bob Dylan, may evade the strife inherent in consciousness, it may evade too our human responsibilities. But this does not alter the fact that some such healing of division within the psyche has been necessary before the new life can be born.

Having attained our rebirth, we should not forget, as Francis Bacon put it, that "the knowledge which induced the Fall was not the natural knowledge of creatures, but the moral knowledge of good and evil, that they had other beginnings, which man aspired to know; to the end to make a total defection from God and to depend wholly upon himself." This defection would be at once a tragedy and a triumph, as was foreseen by Shakespeare, who foresaw most things. In *The Tempest* his Prospero is post-Renaissance man, drunk with knowledge and power, able to reverse the seasons, make brave rivers run retrograde, bring the dead to life, split the atom, blow us all up. Scared at last of the power he hasn't the wisdom to use, he burns his book and casts his wand back to the ooze of the unconscious from which it came. But this is not, and cannot be, an opting out, only an admission that there are things both without and within man's nature which can never be finally mastered. We cannot "know ourselves" unless we can first recognize and accept the fish-like Caliban within us, who was (we recall) an offspring of the Moon-Goddess. Only when we have said, "this Thing of darkenesse I Acknowledge mine" (which may be the task of a lifetime), may we hope to enter into and to possess our brave

A CHART OF RELATIONSHIPS

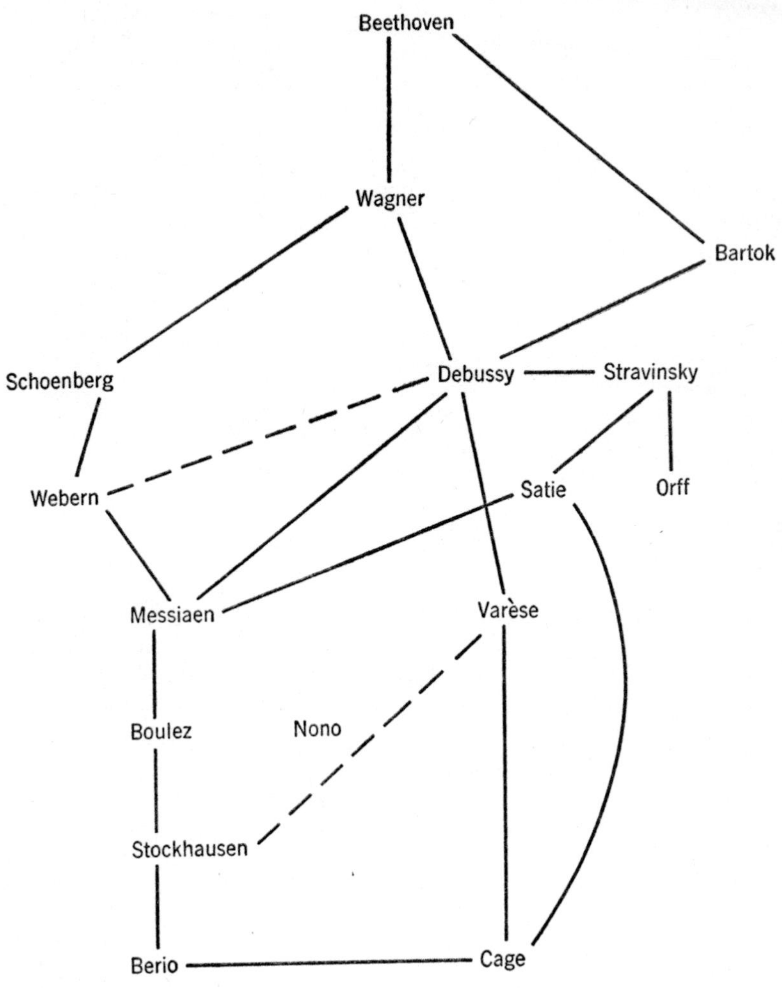

A Note on Editions

of the works analyzed in detail

All the works of Schoenberg and Webern are published by Universal Edition

Debussy's *Pelléas et Mélisande*	Durand et fils
Satie's *Parade*	Edition Salabert
All the works of Orff	Schott and Co.
Stravinsky's *The Wedding*	J. and W. Chester
All the other Stravinsky works	Boosey and Hawkes
Messiaen's *Cinq Rechants* and other works	Rouart Lerolle
The works of Boulez and Stockhausen	Universal Edition
The works of Varèse	Ricordi and Co.
The works of Cage, Feldman and Brown	Peters Edition
Berio's *Circles* and other works	Universal Edition
Britten's *Noye's Fludde*	Boosey and Hawkes
Britten's *Curlew River*	Faber Music
The works of Maxwell Davies here discussed (His later music is published by Boosey and Hawkes.)	Schott and Co.

Glossary

added sixth (Debussyan). A chord consisting of a major triad with the sixth degree of the scale added (e.g., C-E-G-A).

Aeolian (mode). A scale represented by the white keys of the piano beginning on A.

appoggiatura. A dissonant ornamental note, especially common in eighteenth-century music, which resolves on to a concord, the dissonance taking the stress.

aria (da capo). A characteristic form of the eighteenth century, consisting of a melody often of 16 or 32 bars; followed by a middle section in a related key (usually the tonic minor or the relative major); and rounded off by a strict repetition of the first section, usually with additional, often improvised, ornamentation.

arioso. A passage of declamatory or recitative-like character which is none the less to be sung or played lyrically: i.e., halfway between recitative and aria.

atonality. Music without a defined key center.

augmentation. Restatement of a theme (or rhythm) in longer note values.

blue notes. Flattened thirds and sevenths occurring in the blues, within major tonalities; though to describe them as "flattened" is misleading, since they are survivals of vocally modal ways of singing which conflict with modern instrumental tonality.

break (in jazz). An improvised cadenza-like passage, "breaking" across the beat.

canon. Strict imitation of a single theme in a number of different parts. Canons may also be by inversion (the sequence of pitches turned upside down, so that a rising sixth because a falling sixth) or, more rarely, backwards (starting at the end of the theme) or backwards and inverted.

cantus firmus. A pre-existing melody, usually plainsong, used as a basis for a composition. The other parts may or may not be related to the cantus firmus.

chromatic. A scale consisting entirely of semitones; known only in western music.

density (harmonic). A great deal of harmonic activity occurring in a short space, as in Bach's or Schoenberg's music. In this sense Debussy's music is seldom harmonically dense, and Carl Orff's never!

diatonic. Usually applied to the equal-tempered major and minor scales of western Europe.

diminution. Restatement of a theme or rhythm in shorter note values.

dirt (in jazz). Singing or blowing off-pitch, and in other ways exploiting noise, rather than "musical" sound, for expressive purposes.

dorian mode. A scale represented by the white notes on the piano starting on D.

fugato. Imitative passages in a musical texture, though the imitation need not be strictly canonic (see canon).

gagaku. Ancient Japanese court music of high sophistication.

gamalan orchestra. Balinese and Javanese bands of percussion instruments, some pitched, some unpitched.

heterophony. Literally, music in heterogeneous parts, put together without reference to their harmonic implications. Most commonly heterophony consists of different versions of the same melody sung or played simultaneously.

hocquet. A device in late medieval music whereby a passage is broken by rests, regardless of the words. The term is derived from hiccup.

homophony. Music in homogeneous parts; i.e., normally with a tune at the top and the other parts accompanying harmonically.

isochronous motet. A late medieval form in which one part (or more) has a preordained rhythmic pattern which is adhered to throughout, though the pitches change.

just intonation. Singing or playing in the "natural" scales derived from the harmonic series, not in scales artificially fixed by keyboard instruments tuned in Equal Temperament.

klangfarben. A fragmented style of instrumentation especially associated with Webern, whereby each note of a melody may be given a different instrumental color.

leitmotiv. A short theme associated by Wagner with particular characters or ideas, and developed symphonically.

Machaut, Guillaume de. Late medieval composer, c. 1300–1377.

mediant. The third degree of the scale.

melisma. An ornamental passage, especially in oriental and medieval monody; strictly speaking, on a single syllable, though the term is used for any decorative arabesque.

microtonal. Interval smaller than a semitone.

mixolydian mode. A scale represented by the white keys of the piano starting on G.

mode, modality. The fundamental tonal formulae of music, derived from the behavior of the human voice, independent of artificial systems of tuning.

monody, monophony. Music in a single line of melody.

organum. A medieval form of part singing, mainly in parallel fourths and fifths.

ostinato. Melodic figure and/or rhythm insistently repeated.

passacaglia. A composition built over an ostinato, usually in the bass and usually in triple time. Especially favored by composers of the baroque era.

pedal note. A note sustained throughout a developing musical texture, usually though not necessarily in the bass.

pentatonic. Five-note scales; the most rudimentary of all the modes, and the commonest all over the world, because most directly derived from the Harmonic Series.

Perotin. Medieval composer, chapel master at Notre Dame in the twelfth century.

plagal cadence. A progression from subdominant to tonic.

polyphony. Literally, music in many voices; in current usage, music in more than one voice.

ritornello. In the seventeenth century, a short instrumental piece played recurrently during the course of a stage work; later it was applied to the instrumental interludes between vocal sections of an aria or anthem.

rondo. A musical form based on the recurrence of a theme, each recurrence being separated by an episode. In later developments of the rondo, what happens in the episodes tends to modify the theme or its harmonization; this type of developing rondo may be called incremental.

serialism. In chromatic serial music as used by Schoenberg, each note of the composition (chords as well as melodic lines) must be derived from a preordained sequence, or "row," of the twelve chromatic semitones, either in the row's original form, or inverted, or backwards, or backwards and inverted. The serial principle is extended by later composers (Boulez, Stockhausen) to rhythm (or rather metrical proportions), dynamics and timbre (the allocation of notes in the series to different instruments). Though never carried out systematically before the twentieth century, serialism is not a new principle. The medieval cantus firmus acts as a (non-chromatic) row, medieval isochronous motets are rhythmically serial, the ragas and talas of Indian music are more like melodic and rhythmic rows than they are like scales or themes.

subdominant. The fourth degree of the diatonic scale, or the key associated with that note.

tonality. Strictly speaking, the relationships between tones that are inherent in acoustical facts, so that the term covers all scale systems, or rather formulae, from the pentatonic to the chromatic. In practice, however, the word tonality has become associated with the tempered diatonic (major and minor) scales of European music in the eighteenth and nineteenth centuries. The terms atonality and pantonality are used to define the breakdown of that system.

triad. The "common" chord of three notes based on the tonic note with the third and fifth.

tritone. The interval of the augmented fourth or diminished fifth (e.g., B to E sharp or B to F natural). In the Middle Ages it was known as the *Diabolus in musica* because it tended to destroy tonal order, being difficult to sing as a melodic progression and harmonically inimical to the perfect fifth which, to medieval people, was a musical synonymm for God. (Scientifically, the fifth is the most perfect of harmonic relationships after the octave, which is hardly a harmony at all.)

Index